Catholics
—— in the ——
Kitchen

Catholics
in the
Kitchen

*Nurturing the
Bond between
Faith and Food*

Alexandra Greeley

Cover and interior design by Caroline K. Green

Cover and interior images: Shutterstock

Library of Congress Control Number: 2022943624

ISBN: 978-1-5051-2016-5
Kindle ISBN: 978-1-5051-2012-7
ePUB ISBN: 978-1-5051-2017-2

Published in the United States by
TAN Books
PO Box 269
Gastonia, NC 28053
www.TANBooks.com

Printed in the United States of America

Contents

Chefs & Cooks

Cookbook Authors

Author's Note

Catholics in the food world are numerous, even countless. That number includes farmers, chefs, priests, cookbook authors, restaurant owners, and at-home cooks. All of them not only embrace and live their faith but also head to the kitchen to cook for friends, families, parishioners, and the homeless. Some stand in front of a TV camera to broadcast a food show; others head to their computers to write cookbooks and contribute to Catholic websites. Others own and cook for their restaurants and, when time allows, conduct cooking classes to help shape students' techniques and knowledge of ingredients and cooking utensils. Still others—the priests—dream up parish food events or make sure the homeless or the homebound have sufficient food to nourish the body.

Especially important in the food world, of course, are the farmers. Without their skills and labor and dedication to the land, to their crops, and to their herds of animals or flocks of turkeys and chickens, no farmer's market, supermarket, or website food source would have any product or produce to sell. That's why all of us—in this country, in every country—should give thanks to all the farmers in rural communities who work so hard to produce the food to sustain their fellow man.

Fortunately, reaching out to these nineteen profiled Catholics was easy. I write about food and faith for the *National Catholic Register,* and all except one I had already interviewed, as each has a significant role in the food world. They gave me permission for a lengthier profile and a longer phone interview. Of course, fitting time into each person's busy schedule was challenging, so I am grateful to them all. I also extend my gratitude to the Register for allowing me to reprint parts of my original interviews here.

In the end, what has been and is most inspiring, most gratifying, and most challenging are all the eclectic, somewhat universal, and very creative recipes culinary Catholics come up with. Imagine seeing a Burmese recipe for a pineapple-and-tomato soup, for Korean bulgogi (marinated thinly sliced beef steak), or for Italian lentil-and-rice soup. But that's the delight of the universality of the Catholic food world. Catholicism and love of cooking draw in people from all corners of the earth who delight in assembling delicious dishes to feed others, and to feed the soul.

This book, *Catholics in the Kitchen*, focuses on those people from each corner of the American cooking world, starting with the farmers. And that is why the book is dedicated to James Ennis, executive director of Catholic Rural Life, an organization dedicated to "promoting Catholic life in rural America." Readers will also learn about so many different people who use their cooking talents to celebrate life and their faith. Learning about their devotion to God should inspire everyone to thank Him for our life-sustaining food.

Alexandra Greeley

Introduction

*"Know that even when you are in the kitchen,
God moves amidst the pots and pans."*

—SAINT TERESA OF AVILA—

There is a peculiar passage in the book of Acts that could prove difficult to understand if one did not take the time to study the circumstances and context surrounding it. It is a passage that dramatically changed the course of the apostles' evangelization efforts and strategies.

The moment in question concerns the adventures of Peter as he traversed the lands of Lydda, where he healed a bedridden man, followed by his time in Joppa, where he raised a dead woman. Shortly after these miracles, while Peter remained in Joppa, he went up on a housetop to pray. At the sixth hour, he became hungry and "desired something to eat." While his hosts went about preparing a meal, Peter fell into a trance and saw a vision: "The heaven opened, and something descending, like a great sheet, let down by four corners upon the earth. In it were all kinds of animals and reptiles and birds of the air. And there came a voice to him, 'Rise, Peter; kill and eat.' But Peter said, 'No, Lord; for I have never eaten anything that is common or unclean.' And the voice came to him again a second time, 'What God has cleansed you must not call common.' This happened three times, and the thing was taken up at once to heaven" (Acts 10:11–16).

While Peter sat pondering this strange vision, messengers from a centurion named Cornelius called out to him. They had been sent by Cornelius to retrieve Peter, the former having been directed by an angel of God to seek out the latter. Though a pagan, a Roman, and a Gentile Cornelius was an honorable man who "feared God with all his household." The angel had told him to listen to what Peter had to say.

Peter, up until this point, would not have preached much to the Gentiles. And he certainly would not have entered their house to break bread with them, since their food and therefore their bodies would be unclean. But he heard the voice of the Spirit say to him, "Rise and go down, and accompany them without hesitation; for I have sent them" (Acts 10:20).

The next day, Peter obeyed the voice of the Spirit and went to Cornelius. He said to this household, "You yourselves know how unlawful it is for a Jew to associate with or to visit any one of another nation; but God has shown me that I should not call any man common or unclean. So when I was sent for, I came without objection. I ask then why you sent for me" (Acts 10:28–29).

As it turned out, Cornelius desired to hear the story of Jesus. He desired baptism, to be brought into Christ's Church. And he would be that day at the hands of the one Jesus called "the rock."

Sometime later, now in Jerusalem, Peter was criticized by the Jews who demanded an answer for why he would sit at the table with unclean Gentiles. After reciting his vision to them, he argued, "Who was I that I could withstand God?" And when the Jews understood, they glorified God, saying, "Then to the Gentiles also God has granted repentance unto life" (Acts 10:17–18).

And so the Gentiles would be brought into the Church, and so too would all of us, their descendants. Thanks be to God Peter was hungry that day!

All humor aside, this is a vitally important passage for us to reflect on.

For centuries, God had partitioned off His chosen people with a strict set of laws, ensuring they would not mingle with other nations. They had to come to Jerusalem, to the Temple, to gather as a people for the major feasts. There were laws of circumcision, keeping them from marrying and procreating with the Gentiles. And of course there were dietary restrictions, which kept them from dining with "unclean peoples." If one could not worship, marry, or dine with another, it was difficult to mix their cultures or their families. God placed the Jewish people in a cocoon so He could prepare them for the Messiah. We might say this was God playing defense. He was protecting His people from outside threats (though of course He would let these threats target His people when they fell into sin and idolatry).

But the strategy changed after Christ came.

Suddenly, God's people were put on offense. They were told to "go out and make disciples of all nations." No longer would circumcision be the law, but baptism. No longer would they gather in the Temple, shutting themselves off, but tabernacles would be spread out all over the world, inviting all who sought the Lord to come in. And, as we saw with the vision of Peter in Acts, the Jewish dietary laws would also be lifted. Peter and the other Christians could now sit at the table with Gentiles. They could dine with them.

It's probably not all that surprising that the manner in which God's people worshiped Him, as well as the joining of families through marriage to create new families, would be vitally important to the conversion of the Gentiles. But we see how sacred the act of sitting down to dine with someone is when we consider this was also a means of conversion desired by God. He knew that the human family—His children—shared more than just food when they ate together. They shared their spirits with one another. They shared love.

Thus, the Spirit counseled Peter, and through Peter the other apostles, to break bread with the Gentiles, for the Spirit knew what they did not—that in the breaking of common bread, the Jews and the Gentiles would soon consume the heavenly Bread together as well.

★   ★   ★

The life of the family and the community more broadly is incredibly dependent upon sharing meals together. This is an area of human life we take for granted until we stop and force ourselves to appreciate it. The dinner table is where we come to know one another, whether it be strangers meeting for the first time, or a married couple of sixty years, or a big, chaotic family. Without the act of eating and drinking, our time together is diminished and can even seem hollow or sterile.

Picture those strangers. Perhaps they're meeting in the office about business. A potential deal might be struck. The talk is cordial throughout the morning, but stiff. Purely business. Each is sizing the other up, wondering where the other stands. Then they go to lunch. A meal is shared. Suddenly the conversation becomes more friendly, more familiar. They talk of their families, of their pasts, maybe their interests. A few jokes are cracked. The food and drink on the table before them has broken down the wall of unfamiliarity. Now that they have shared a meal, there is more of a bond, even if only a small one. Food has brought them together.

Now picture that married couple. They sit watching the news in the early evening. Together in the den, both stare at the television screen. Dialogue is scant. The television is the center of attention. Suddenly, they are hungry. It is time to start dinner preparations. The TV is turned off and they move into the kitchen. Pleasant aromas begin to fill the house: warm steam, tomato sauce, and garlic. The sounds of pots and pans banging together and timers going off enliven the atmosphere. Each is doing something to serve the other. She strains the noodles. He sets the table and fills the water glasses. They sit, bless their food, and begin to eat. They begin to talk. Even after sixty years, they fail to tire of each other's company at the table. They may not appreciate it fully now, but when one of them is gone, this moment at the table is what will be missed, not watching the news.

Now the family: Mom, Dad, three boys, and four girls. The outside world can't believe they have that many kids. But they do. How do you do it all? Isn't it chaotic? Yes, it is. Work pulls at mom and dad in different capacities.

Kids are off to school, to sports, to piano, or to a friend's house. The dog is sick. What is that ominous sound bellowing from the belly of the washer? But the day is nearing an end. Dusk falls outside. Everyone is finally under the roof again. Preparations begin in the kitchen. Smells, sounds, and tastes abound. The kids pitch in, the older ones anyway, setting the table. Don't forget to put the top on Timmy's cup! They all sit when the meal is ready. After a blessing, conversation and laughter ensues. Someone got an A in math. Someone hit a double. Someone's nervous for her piano recital tomorrow. Though all were scattered throughout the day, all are now gathered. As a family.

These are ordinary settings. But food is just as vital at the major feasts of life. At Halloween, children want something sweet to eat, while extended family gather for Thanksgiving and Christmas, centering their time around the dinner table. We eat at weddings, gathering around when the cake is cut. At wakes, we all bring food, making extra casseroles for the departed's family, manifesting our love, our sympathy, and our compassion. Going out to dinner is a special treat, done often to mark anniversaries.

The human body is dependent on food to survive. But human relationships are just as dependent on it. This includes the bond between generations. The passing down of recipes from grandmother to mother to daughter links past, present, and future, right there in the kitchen amidst the pots and the pans. Fathers and sons, brothers and uncles, drink beer by the grill, talking about the game. Lunchtime at school is when childhood friends are made, some that last a lifetime, and parish fish fries at Lent build up the local community.

Food also nurtures our relationship to the land. Hunters take pride in literally bringing in their dinner from the wild, and perhaps no hobby is more of a balm for the soul than gardening, growing one's own vegetables in the backyard. Even those of us who don't know the first thing about milking a cow have romantic aspirations of life on the farm. Why is this? Because when we go directly to the source for our food, cutting out the chain stores, we come closer to the Source from which all life comes. Whether we know it or not, this is the attraction to hunting, to gardening, and to farming. They lead us to God.

★ ★ ★

Every generation has a tendency to think that theirs is living in the end times. Nothing could be as bad as this, we tell ourselves. There is no doubt a bit of pride in that narrowly biased belief. Nonetheless, we should acknowledge the downfall of civilization when we see it before our eyes. And much has come before our eyes these days.

There is no need to go into detail, but a quick list of the devil's recent impressive work includes world wars, abortion, divorce, pornography and widespread sexual deviancy, a decrease in church attendance, a staggering rise in depression and suicides, militant secularism, and devastating scandals within Holy Mother Church to name just a few. The reasons for this dark list are many and complicated, and this is not the time and place to discuss them. What *is* pertinent here is to show that, not coincidentally, our food life has also crumbled in recent times, moving right alongside our moral poverty.

Eating is certainly not a sin. But gluttony is. The hitherto praise given to food and the act of eating should not be confused with the worship of food. All the circumstances just described centered on food bringing loved ones together, bringing us into harmony with nature, and ultimately, bringing us to God. Conversely, gluttony is the worship of food. It is an overindulgence of food and drink, wanting too much of it or taking improper pleasure in it, placing that pleasure above all else, including God.

Today, our food is sugary, sweet, greasy, fatty, and processed. Our obesity statistics today would be unconscionable to past generations. (In all the black and white photos from the past, have you ever seen a person grossly overweight?) We are tempted toward eating bad food because it is so readily available, with seven fast food joints off each highway exit, and forty-six different types of sugary cereal on aisle five. We snack so much throughout the day that when we sit down for a meal, it doesn't feel all that special. Temptation to gluttony abounds, but we often overlook these temptations, more so than we do with temptations to lust, which present themselves far more acutely.

Considering that we seem to be stricken with collective amnesia when it comes to appreciating the good, the true, and the beautiful, it is no wonder that our approach to food has similarly been cheapened, compromised, and robbed of its wholesomeness and purpose. It feels, unfortunately, similar to lust, to what has happened to the natural love that can be exchanged between man and woman, between husband and wife. Sex is a gift from God, as is the act of eating. But both have been corrupted, placing the desire for pleasure over the beauty and true purpose of the act.

Beyond the corruption of our food, the act of eating bringing people together has also faded. The family dinner is sacrosanct and the diminishing of it has contributed greatly to the disintegration of family life in the home and thus the culture more broadly. Life is too hectic now for families to share meals. Couples eat in front of the television. The professionals downtown, instead of striking up a conversation with a stranger, stare at phones while they wait in line for their lunch at the deli, as well as when they go to eat it. Students, too, stare at their phones instead of striking up new friendships in the campus cafeteria.

Like in so many other areas of life, we have lost control of our appetites. The inevitable result of that is to turn inward on ourselves, seeking to satisfy the self and losing our communion with others.

★   ★   ★

The nineteen individuals featured in this work have spent a lifetime trying to turn back the tide of this downward spiral that has buried our heads in the pig trough (and rectangular flashing screens). They have sought to heal our societal indigestion, if only in small ways, in their families and local communities.

They are farmers, ranchers, chefs, cooks, professors, authors, moms, dads, grandparents, and priests.

They own cafés, restaurants, and farm stores. They have their own cooking shows, their own blogs. They've penned cookbooks and founded organizations and movements. They teach cooking classes and feed the homeless. They raise and, when the time comes, slaughter livestock. They've worked for major food corporations and served musicians, celebrities, ambassadors, and dignitaries. They have appeared on the Food Network, EWTN, and the Catholic Faith Network. They studied their crafts in Paris, Rome, and the Holy Land.

They come from different regions—from Colorado to rural Virginia to the Louisiana Bayou—and from difficult cultures—Latino, Polish, Lebanese, Italian, and Irish, among others.

It is a wide palette of humanity. And yet, the one ingredient found in all of them is the Catholic faith. Some are cradle Catholics, some converts, and some reverts. Their faith journeys are as myriad as their backgrounds and favorite dishes. But each of them call Holy Mother Church their home.

Perhaps this should come as no surprise. While all cultures and faiths value gathering at the table with family and friends, the culinary arts were borne from Catholic culture in France and in Italy. For centuries, monks were the ones who not only taught us how to cultivate the land, but how to make wine and excellent beer. No one has ever accused Catholics of championing a puritanical diet. We Catholics take what the Lord has made, these things He called "good," and celebrate them as He intended us to. But just as the Church does in all things, she oversees our use of these natural goods and orders them not toward overindulgence or excessive pleasure but toward our sanctification, seeing them as a taste of the heavenly banquet to come.

These nineteen Catholics, no matter who they are, have sought to show others the profound connection between food and faith, to show us that eating is a moral act in more ways than one. The act of growing food, of tending the land and caring for animals, of serving others and passing down recipes, for all of them these are a means to love others and to love God. Their love of food has carried them through difficult times, led them to their spouse, given them a sense of peace, put them on a path back to God, and supported their families for decades.

And here in these pages they have shared with us their favorite dishes, from tilapia to oyster gumbo, from chicken creole to butternut squash soup, from beef steaks and goetta to fizzy tea and "resurrection rolls." Still there's more: potato-leek soup, orecchiette, tabbouleh, and hunter's stew. And for dessert, how does Polish cream cake sound?

Yet beyond the recipes, they show us too how a life close to the land, a life in the kitchen serving others, a life around the table with family and friends, is a life that leads to heaven.

★ ★ ★

Poets have described the Sacred Mass as the place where earth and heaven kiss. This is a beautiful image that helps us realize there is no more important time for a Catholic than time spent at Mass. And let us not forget that the Mass is patterned after a family meal. Just as we gather with family to talk and eat, at Mass we gather with the Body of Christ to talk (the Liturgy of the Word) and eat (the Liturgy of the Eucharist).

This family meal, though, is not just for your family or the one down the street but for the entire world, both geographically and temporally. Geographically because the Church's maternal arms reach to the four corners of the world; temporally because the Mass is a re-presentation of the Last Supper and Christ's sacrifice on Calvary. This means it "makes present again" these sacred moments. It is as if the Mass is a time portal that opens us up to the Passion, the most important event in history. It is God's way of bringing His children together at His table to partake of the banquet that sustains our souls.

Have we considered the miracle that is the Mass? That this human body, so torn by violence and hate, by conflict and confusion, let alone separated by continents and centuries, could carry out a tradition all across the globe for over two millennia without interruption? Does this universal family meal not prove the divinity of the Church?

At its core, this book in your hands is a cookbook. We hope that you will take some of these recipes and make them a part of your family traditions. But more than that this book is a collection of human-interest stories, stories that are interesting, yes, but still not all that much different than your own. These are just ordinary people striving to reach heaven. We hope you find them inspiring and that in some small way this book leads you to God, that it takes you from the dining room table to the altar, that it feeds your body, but more so, your soul.

Editor, TAN Books

Farmers

A Champion for Catholic Rural Life

James Ennis

"God Was Fifth in My Life"

There is a proverb in the Old Testament that says, "A man's mind plans his way, but the LORD directs his steps" (Prv 16:9). This is certainly true in the life of James Ennis, executive director for Catholic Rural Life, an organization based in St. Paul, Minnesota, that works to promote Catholic life in rural America.[1]

James Ennis

"I remember it as if it were yesterday. In the spring of my freshman year in college at the University of California at Davis," he recalls. "I was sick and tired of my partying lifestyle. One night I ran up to the roof of my dormitory and cried out to God and asked Him to reveal Himself to me."

A week later, he was invited to a Bible study group. "When my buddies on my floor asked where I was going that evening, I flippantly told them, 'To a BS session.' During that first evening, the instructor asked us to list the top priorities. I listed school, family, girlfriend, other friends, and faith. God was fifth in my life. The instructor then shared Matthew 6:33 with all of us: 'But seek first God's kingdom and God's righteousness, and all these things shall be yours as well.'"

Afterwards, troubled by the verse, Ennis met with the instructor for lunch. Over a meal, Ennis asked several questions about faith and how to put God first in one's life.

"Even though I had heard the Gospel reading every Sunday at Mass, I viewed my Catholicism as a religion, not a *relationship* with God," Ennis said. "I asked the instructor how I could establish a relationship with God."

---

[1] For more information, go to the Catholic Rural Life website at https://catholicrurallife.org.

That was the beginning of his faith coming alive. "I felt like I was seeing things I had never seen before. I was more well-disposed to Christ and all he had to say, and it changed how I was and how I treated people."

An Irish Home

A cradle Catholic born in Southern California, Ennis grew up in a devout Irish Catholic family who attended Mass regularly. Ennis's eventual interest in the food world began during childhood while he watched his mother cook. As he noted, coming from an Irish Catholic family means relying on eating traditional Irish dishes, such as meals featuring meat and potatoes with a side salad.

"My mom was a great cook, and she prepared everything mostly from scratch. She loved making meat loaf and ham, and our regular fare was really geared to a large family on a budget. We had tuna casseroles, and with five boys and one girl, she had to really spread it. I loved her oatmeal and chocolate chip cookies, all of which she made from scratch. And her pie crusts were great."

He recalls that his dad also cooked, primarily grilling hamburgers and hot dogs out in the backyard. But the real pull for Ennis was his mother's meals. "I watched her while she cooked. I learned to peel and mash potatoes and became involved in food preparation."

As a teenager, Ennis worked summers at the local fire department. One of his duties was to cook for the crew on duty. Working away in the station kitchen, he often ended up on the phone with his mother, asking her about steps, ingredients, and timing.

"As a young adult, I cooked a lot, and a lot of what I cooked was what Mom taught me."

Ennis studied agricultural economics in college and learned much about our national food system. All that laid the groundwork for his eventual leadership role in Catholic Rural Life and his passion for cooking.

African Influence

Ennis's life took a significant detour after that night at the Bible study his freshman year. He eventually got involved in student ministry through a Protestant organization. That led him to becoming a missionary on the campus of the University of Zambia in Africa for two years.

In Zambia, Ennis learned a very different way to cook from his Irish food memories. "The staple food in Zambia was maize meal. For breakfast, I mixed maize meal in boiling water to the consistency of Malt-O-Meal hot cereal and served it with bread and tea. For lunch and dinner, I added more maize meal into boiling water to make *nshima*, the consistency of which was very similar to thick mashed potatoes. I would add a side dish of beef or fish in a tomato sauce and some fried vegetables. I used a lot of cooking oil. I would go to the local market to buy cooking oil, maize, meat, and vegetables. That was all from scratch. I ate pretty basic food but ate well."

Though he wouldn't realize it until later, Ennis came to see that his Zambian cooking experiences had firmly influenced his passion for food and cooking.

Coming Home Again

When he returned to the United States, he entered graduate school. "I went to the University of Minnesota for an MBA. I met a lot of graduate students from all over the world. And I would host friends, invite them over to my house, and we would cook from scratch. I learned many different dishes— Indian, Filipino, Indonesian. I did that for two years."

After graduate school, Ennis worked for six years in corporate marketing for two different food companies: Pillsbury, where he was assigned to the Green Giant brand, and The Clorox Company, where he was assigned to several brands, including Hidden Valley Ranch products. He eventually moved into the nonprofit world and worked for Cooperative Development Services with its ties to farmers and farmer-owned cooperatives nationwide.

"My work was in the food world in a secular position. I spoke around the country about sustainable agriculture. At some of the conferences I attended, I was troubled by what some speakers asserted concerning environmental degradation and its causes, that Christians were a culprit due to their misinterpretation of the command in Genesis to 'tend and to till the earth.'"

During this period, Ennis's family life changed dramatically. "I met my wife, Sally, while visiting a friend in Virginia. Sally was a widow with two young daughters, ages five and six. We married and eventually had three more children. When we both became troubled by some things at the church we were attending at that time, we began a search for a new church home. That search eventually led us to examine the Catholic Church once again."

While visiting relatives in St. Louis one Christmas, Ennis's brother-in-law gave him Scott Hahn's book *Rome Sweet Home*, a story about Hahn's journey to Catholicism. Ennis read the book over the weekend and discovered the plausibility structure he needed to return to the Church. Over the next two years, Ennis and Sally read several biographies about people's journeys to Catholicism, in addition to early Church writings. All of this led Jim to re-enter the Church, and the rest of the Ennis family was received on the Easter Vigil of 2002.

Catholic Rural Life

Several years later, while at a dinner party in 2006, Ennis met a moral theologian from the Saint Paul Seminary. "I had just read Pope John Paul II's *Theology of the Body*, and I needed a *Theology of Creation* on the environment. As it turned out, this particular theologian was working on a book very much like that!"

The theologian went on to say, "A lot of Catholics suffer from a 'Nature Deficit Disorder,' a blindness towards the environment. Many view the environment as simply something to use. We are part of creation, and all of us need to see it and treat it as gift." That conversation began a significant long-term collaboration between the two men that continues to this day.

The Lord also opened a door for Ennis in 2008 when a position opened up at Catholic Rural Life (formerly National Catholic Rural Life Conference). Ennis applied for the position and was offered the job.

"I became the executive director and joined an organization that has been applying the Church's teachings to rural life for over ninety-eight years."

The organization has had a profound impact on rural farmers in the past, and Ennis decided to help redevelop the network of rural priests and farmers around the country and to help promote the Catholic life in rural America.

In the late 1990s, the then-director, Brother David Andrews of the National Catholic Rural Life Conference, developed a campaign entitled "Why eating is a moral act."

"He wanted to build a bridge with consumers to put trust in the food system," said Ennis. "He asked the important questions: 'How can we ensure a safe, affordable, and sustainable food supply? How can we preserve the land and the water while providing food for our nation?'" In 2003, the United States Conference of Catholic Bishops wrote a letter to all Catholics articulating the Church's teachings on why food production is a moral issue, giving credence to the mission of the Rural Life Conference.

From its roots, said Ennis, the organization's focus has been on evangelization, education, and promoting Catholic life in rural America. Catholic Rural Life's vision is one of a flourishing Catholic life in rural America: thriving families, farms, and parishes that are centered on faith, community,

and care of creation. Its work in ethical agriculture and rural ministry supports and builds the rural Church by educating clergy, religious, and lay leaders.

Ennis noted that prior to Pope John Paul II's trip to the United States in October of 1979, an Iowan farmer invited the pope to come to Iowa and speak to rural America. The pope accepted the invitation and added Iowa to his itinerary. Hosted by Catholic Rural Life, the Diocese of Des Moines, and Living History Farms, the pope spoke to over three hundred thousand people, many of whom were farmers, about caring for the land and being good stewards of God's earth. That was the first time that a pope spoke publicly to American farmers about their responsibility to be good stewards of the land.

Today, approximately 17 percent of the US population (fifty to sixty million people) live in rural communities. There are approximately 2.1 million farmers in the United States—down 50 percent from 1960—who provide food for the country. There are also many environmental concerns about soil, water and air pollution in rural America that are related to agricultural production.

As Ennis said, "I work at Catholic Rural Life because it's where I can live out my passion for Christ and His Church and also get to work with farmers and ranchers from around the country. The Catholic Church affirms all who are involved in agricultural production and who help bring food to our tables."

Of course, when he is not traveling or speaking at conferences, Ennis, along with his wife, Sally, enjoy time at home. "Sally and I both enjoy cooking—she in the kitchen and me outside on the grill. One of our favorite dishes is pork tenderloin marinated in a sauce for several hours before grilling. I also enjoy grilling fish, especially salmon, and chicken, barbecue ribs, hamburgers, steaks, and shish kabobs. We grill often during the summer months. Even during the winter, we try to grill outdoors once a week. Sally and I both love the outdoors and camping, and cooking food over a grill reminds us of some of our favorite getaways when we go camping on Lake Superior."

Ina Garten's Herb-Marinated Pork Tenderloins

James Ennis said that this is one of his favorite meat entrées, and one he and his wife cook for gatherings. Packed with flavor, the dish is easy to assemble and cooks up quickly. It is a recipe attributed to popular chef Ina Garten.

SERVES 8

Ingredients:

- 1 lemon, zest grated
- ¾ cup freshly squeezed lemon juice
- Olive oil
- 2 tablespoons minced garlic (6 cloves)
- 1 ½ tablespoons minced fresh rosemary
- 1 tablespoon chopped fresh thyme leaves
- 2 teaspoons Dijon mustard
- Kosher salt
- 3 pork tenderloins, about 1 pound each
- Freshly ground black pepper

Directions:

1. Combine the lemon zest, lemon juice, ½ cup olive oil, garlic, rosemary, thyme, mustard, and 2 teaspoons salt in a sturdy 1-gallon resealable plastic bag.
2. Add the pork tenderloins and turn to coat with the marinade. Squeeze out the air and seal the bag. Marinate the pork in the refrigerator for at least 3 hours but preferably overnight.
3. Preheat grill to 400 degrees F.
4. Remove the tenderloins from the marinade and discard the marinade but leave the herbs clinging to the meat.
5. Sprinkle the tenderloins generously with salt and pepper.
6. Cook the pork tenderloins on all sides until golden brown (5 minutes per side of four sides). Continue to cook the tenderloins for 5–10 minutes or until the meat registers 137 degrees F at the thickest part.
7. Transfer the tenderloins to a platter and cover each tenderloin with aluminum foil. Allow to rest for 10 minutes.
8. Carve in ½-inch-thick diagonal slices. The thickest part of the tenderloin will be quite pink (it's just fine) and the thinnest part will be done.
9. Season with salt and pepper and serve warm, or at room temperature with the juices that collect in the platter.

The Queen
of Athenry

Elaine Boland

A Lesson Learned

Due to her outstanding cooking skills, people who know Elaine Boland figure she can prepare just about anything. And she can. But one night, she learned an important lesson.

Elaine Boland

She had just finished cooking a lamb chili to sell in her farm store, along with several other stews and dishes. It had been a hectic day, and when she finished the last batch, it was nearly midnight. Instead of waking her husband to help carry the full pots downstairs to the refrigerator, Elaine figured she could do it herself.

"Down the stairs I most certainly went!" she recalls with a smile, one surely not present at the time. "Tripping, bouncing off the walls and stairs all the way down. Broken ribs! Chili everywhere, floor to ceiling and around the bend! Need I say more? The moral of this story: Know your quitting time or ask for help!"

Animals, Faith, and a "Farmette"

As a Cincinnati native, Elaine Boland at sixteen years of age bought her first horse, a two-year-old thoroughbred, from a veterinarian friend and neighbor. The purchase took place without the knowledge of her parents. "I grew up loving animals and was always bringing something home. I hid that horse for two years at my friend's farm before one of my five sisters ratted me out! I was in so much trouble!"

"Eventually our family moved from Cincinnati to Arizona, where we had a 640-acre ranch of Santa Gertrudis cattle and cotton. My horse, Frisco, came with us, named for the San Francisco Peaks in Flagstaff. We had so much fun. I loved those years with him."

In addition to her devotion to animals, Elaine grew up in a fervent Catholic family and, as a result, has always been passionate about her faith. "My Catholic family was very active, and it was really *fun*. Our grade school was St. Vivian, and Fr. Joseph Ratterman was our pastor. I remember he smoked a pipe, and it smelled so good. He was so much fun. Back then, we still had nuns in full habits teaching us. We had the most magnificent choir at St. Vivian's. It was like going to the Vatican it was so brilliant."

Her Catholicism and devotion to animals—and to cooking—have played out in her adult life. When she got married, her brother-in-law and his wife suggested to the couple that they should move to either Middleburg, Leesburg, or Purcellville in Northern Virginia.

The couple chose Purcellville, and that is where Elaine's childhood dream of living on a farm became a reality. They found a country setting. The thirty-acre open space was ideal for raising a family. There the children could run free, and the parents could run their farm, which they named Fields of Athenry.

"The name comes from a close friend, Fr. James McCurry, whose family runs sheep in the true Fields of Athenry, near Galway Bay, in Ireland. Father McCurry is truly special. He has been a dear family friend who baptized all our children and grandchildren and married some of our daughters too. He covers provinces all over the world for the Conventual Franciscans, which is why we lovingly call him 'the walking, talking holy spirit.'"

She added there is an Irish ballad by the name "Fields of Athenry" written by the Irishman Pete St. John. One day, a young man and his wife came driving down the entrance into the farm. It turned out that divine providence had directed Pete St. John's son to drive right past Fields of Athenry on a family trip. He couldn't help but stop when he saw the sign. Elaine, for her part, saw a sign too—a sign that she had given her farm the perfect name!

With the family's move, Elaine was thrilled she could provide a little "farmette" for her children, who were toddlers at the time. She envisioned them romping in the fields and playing with baby lambs. They rode sheep around the farm like ponies while she and her husband raised a few chickens, ducks, and turkeys. The children also enjoyed scavenger hunts and other games in the barn.

As time passed, a contact from the local economic development committee came out to the farm and asked Elaine if she wanted to join the local Purcellville farm market.

"I agreed to, and it was a great decision. Once a week going to the farm market with the kids, those were some cherished memories. I was the only one who went with prepared meals, such as chicken soups. That's how I got my home kitchen inspected early on. I said I liked to cook, and the prepared meals took off. And I sold thirty turkeys that first Thanksgiving there."

Now, years later, she sells around 1,500 turkeys annually.

The Cross of Suffering

Family life took a sad turn when one of her daughters reached first grade and started to unexpectedly gain weight. "She started saying her 'leggies' hurt. Children so often complain of aches and pains so it's easy to overlook those complaints. But then she swelled up and looked like she was gaining weight. Then her belly started to swell, and she would become flush red for no reason. She would also get awful headaches and bruise terribly when she fell off her pony, unlike the other children."

Elaine took her to different doctors searching for a diagnosis. She was told that her daughter's hormones were out of order, or that she was not getting enough exercise, or she was not eating the right diet. "Then a holistic doctor told me I had to focus on nutrition. And the better I fed her, the better she would be. They told me I needed to boost her with organ meats, such as liver, and to make bone broth."

Six-and-a-half years later, her daughter's headaches were so bad and her joint pain so severe that Elaine took her to see an endocrinologist. She was diagnosed with an illness known as Cushing's disease, caused by a tumor in her brain. He told Elaine that a surgeon would have to remove the tumor. The family praised God when the surgery was successful, and though she requires yearly checkups to ensure the tumor has not grown back, they rely on their faith in God to carry them through that experience.

The Fields of Athenry & Side Saddle Bistro

The episode with her daughter's tumor led Elaine to dedicate herself to promoting family health through the concept of nutrient-dense eating. As a start, she read the works of nutritionist Weston A. Price and others, which taught her about the health benefits of soup stocks, and bone broth, made from bones, meats, animal organs, and vegetables simmering for hours. She learned that the whole animal itself, when having lived a completely natural life without chemical-laden grass, creates an animal that can yield true human nutrition.

In addition to cooking healthful meals for her family, Elaine also began to prepare homemade dinners to sell at the farm store she would open called Fields of Athenry & Side Saddle Bistro,[2] which also offers home delivery. Her store stocks soups, stews, chilis, and numerous cuts of meat that customers might not cook at home, such as well-fed sheep, pigs, poultry (including all those turkeys!), and beef cattle. She also sells eggs, honey, butter, cheese, wild-caught fish, and a range of other products.

"I came up with making meals out of these animals from head to tail," she said, using bottom roasts and brisket, cuts that take too long

[2] For more information, visit https://fieldsofathenryfarm.com.

to cook for most busy people. "Early on, I learned to butcher them, first through the USDA, and then I taught myself. I watched food processors and learned from some very knowledgeable people."

Obviously, cooking was always a part of God's plan for her. She grew up in a German-Irish-Dutch family in which both her mother and grandmother were great cooks. "My grandparents had a farm in Ohio. My mom would tell me stories about the animals, how she had to walk so far to school, and she would cut through local farms, and one day a bull chased her right over the fence! My mom loved telling that story."

Where Elaine grew up, there was a field near where they lived that had silver corn. "We would pick it right in the field and eat it, hoping the farmer didn't catch us." And each family meal featured three sturdy courses with meats, vegetables, and a dessert.

Elaine's favorite recipe is a German/ Irish dish called *goetta*, passed down through her family. "It's like a breakfast spread, like a scrapple, made from steel cut oats and sausages. You can freeze the loaf pans and take them out for later."

After decades of farming and with her children grown, Elaine and her husband moved from their first farm to a smaller farm in nearby Middleburg. But they still have land across the street from the Fields of Athenry where they raise hundreds of ducks, geese, and turkeys. She also manages and continues to cook for her farm store that she moved to a new location in the heart of Middleburg.

Though the time spent suffering through her daughter's illness was a time of confusion and pain, Elaine thanks God for the doctors who helped cure her, and for the path He took her family down. The cross of suffering they bore led them to a way of life that has brought them peace and happiness, and even a small taste of earthly success.

"God had plans for us that I never imagined; I never pictured myself doing what I do now. All praise and glory go to Him."

To give Him thanks, she says her prayers daily and attends Mass frequently.

Fields of Athenry Goetta

"Toast your favorite bread and butter your toast! Great Grandma Fette said this is a must! Then spread the goetta on top! Oh, oh yum!" said Boland.

Ingredients:

- 1 pound Fields of Athenry Farm mild pork sausage or other mild pork sausage, crumbled (add 1 to 2 teaspoons ground sage)
- 1 quart water or Fields of Athenry Farm Liquid Gold Baby Broth
- 1 ¼ cups pinhead oatmeal

- 1 small onion, peeled, diced, and sautéed
- 1 bay leaf
- Salt, ground black pepper, and sage to taste

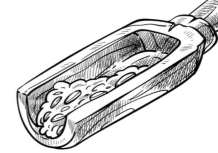

Directions:

1. Crumble the sausage and cook it lightly, adding sage, then squeeze out all the grease by rolling in a paper towel.
2. Add the oats (having mixed with the appropriate amount of water) and onion with bay leaf to the sausage and cook in a Dutch oven on the stove top.
3. Cook on low with the lid cracked for about 1 hour, then place the cooked mixture in a bread loaf pan.
4. Place in a refrigerator for several hours or overnight to become a solid loaf.
5. Take the *goetta* loaf out and slice like a thick cut of butter. Sear to heat in frying pan.

An Advocate
for Farmers
and Ranchers

Mike Callicrate

A Rural Colorado Childhood

Since 1985, America has lost half of its ranchers, but Mike Callicrate is determined to reverse that trend.

Mike Callicrate

Born in Denver and raised in Evergreen, Colorado, Callicrate came from a devout Catholic family with eight children. "We went to Mass every Sunday. And on Saturday mornings, we studied the *Catechism*. Before high school, I was working in a grocery store owned by a Catholic friend of the family. Many of the people I was around were hardworking Catholics, so I grew up with that influence."

His passion for farming began early in life. "When I was growing up, I joined the local 4-H Club.[3] I had a Corriedale sheep project and showed at the Jefferson County fair. Sheep are a great project for young kids; they are less expensive than cattle and easy to work with. Then I got interested in riding bulls, which took me into the rodeo world."

Not surprisingly, Mike's passion for rural issues stems from his family upbringing. "My grandfather was a dry-land tenant farmer in Weld County, Colorado. It was a tough life farming in such a dry place without irrigation, but my dad grew up loving livestock and growing things. My dad became a millwright, working on the Eisenhower Tunnel and other large infrastructure projects in Colorado and across the nation. I learned at an early age the value of growing and making things. We did as much as we could agriculturally on the five acres south of Evergreen, including a garden, chickens, horses, my brother's turkeys, and my 4-H sheep project."

---

[3] 4-H Clubs are for young people and teens to participate in farming and other projects to work together with adult mentors.

A Career in Ranching

After graduating from Colorado State University, Mike went into farming and ranching in St. Francis, Kansas, but soon became discouraged by how little competition there was for his cattle. As the meatpackers became more consolidated, fewer buyers came to his farm and the bids they made were lower and lower. Rather than relying on packers to process and distribute his cattle, he decided to create a more direct path to the marketplace by doing the processing and distribution himself.

As a rancher, he was also working to develop a regenerative production model, diversifying the cattle production with pigs and chickens. "Having a diversity of livestock on the landscape, combined with cover cropping, native tree planting, and other environmental practices, helps to restore the fragile High Plains ecosystem," he explained. "A unique aspect to increase meat quality is our use of Wagyu bulls on Angus females. Wagyu is a Japanese breed of cattle known for having less outer-muscle fat but exceptionally high levels of marbling, or intramuscular fat, which creates rich, buttery meat."[4]

"It takes more than two years of care and investment to get a cut of meat from pasture to plate, he continued. "Most ranchers run cows that produce calves every year, which are then raised on grass or hay until they are ready to be fattened on roughages and grain in the feedlot. From there, they go to a large meat processing plant, which is almost certainly owned by one of four large meatpackers that together process more than 85 percent of the nation's beef."

"But in our operation, the calves never leave the nurturing care of Callicrate Cattle Company. Since 2011, the animals have been processed right at the farm by a small crew working under federal USDA oversight. It's an approach that is still very uncommon, with only a few of these on-farm processing units operating nationwide, but it has generated a groundswell of interest among livestock producers looking for alternatives to the industrial production model."

---

[4] The meat from Wagyu cattle is sometimes referred to as Kobe beef, although technically that term only applies to beef that originates in Kobe, Japan.

Mike went on to explain how their farming prototype could be used to make food more local and sustainable. "Processing on location eliminates the need to haul cattle long distances and greatly reduces their stress level, which also improves meat quality and tenderness. Just as importantly, our animals are fed a healthy ration without any of the artificial growth-promoting substances that have become widely used by large feedlots to rapidly bulk up the musculature of cattle. I always say, what makes our meat so good isn't what we do; it's what we *don't* do."

To market his products, Mike established a carcass processing plant and two retail stores.

"One of the challenges for ranchers who want to market their beef directly to customers is being located in remote rural areas far from urban centers. When I started my business, I knew that in order to reach customers, we would need to set up a market somewhere along the highly populated Front Range of Colorado."

"After exploring the options, I chose to open a market in Colorado Springs in large part because I was doing business with a small local beef processor at the time, which has since closed. Our store is continuing to expand its wide selection of products—which includes Colorado grown lamb, wild-caught Pacific salmon, assorted fresh produce, and many prepared food items—all sourced as directly as possible from other growers, gardeners, farmers, and fishermen."

Customers can buy the meat at the two retail stores he operates in Colorado Springs and online. He also has a food-hub in the processing plant facility that serves as a distribution point for other small regional food producers. Several restaurants partner with Mike, along with small specialty markets. He never sells to chains or franchise restaurants, favoring local independent establishments.

He also markets directly to consumers. "Our meat really is the best there is. We combine high quality breeds with clean natural diets, low-stress on-farm handling and slaughter, proper aging, and expert cutting for the best possible end product."

Mike has worked hard over the years to explain to diverse audiences how food choices are connected to economic and social justice issues. Are farmers being paid a fair price for what they produce? Are workers being treated fairly and not exploited? Is anti-trust enforcement adequate to prevent a few big companies from using their leverage to benefit themselves at the expense of farmers, workers, and consumers? To help explore those questions and tell that story, he served as an advisor for several documentary films, including *Food Inc.*, and popular books like *The Omnivore's Dilemma* and *Fast Food Nation*.

Eating as a Moral Act

He also noted that one of the biggest influences in his life has been the organization Catholic Rural Life, now led by executive director James Ennis (featured in chapter 1). Mike first became familiar with the group and its mission when it was under the direction of former director Br. David Andrews, who is now deceased.

"I really made the connection between food and faith after meeting Br. David Andrews, when he was executive director of

the National Catholic Rural Life Conference. He reinforced my view that eating is a moral act, because our food choices have an impact on farmers, workers, animals, and the environment. I admired him so much, especially his calm demeanor and his dedication to bringing people together, regardless of political views or backgrounds, to work on important social justice issues."

Mike wrote a stirring article for the June 2019 issue of the Catholic Rural Life magazine and website, which stated in part: "My stance on agriculture is an expression of my Catholic faith and the values I was raised with. As a cradle Catholic, I was taught that life and work have a moral dimension and that we are expected to do good things for others and fulfill a role of responsibility in our home and community. Eating truly is a moral act."

Mike feels that local parishes have not done enough to explain the connection between food and faith.

"One of our local parishes in Colorado Springs promoted a fundraiser with a large grocery store chain, encouraging the parishioners to shop there, excluding small locally owned craft butchers like myself who are creating skilled jobs and keeping the profits in the local community. Big chain retailers are intent on driving down prices to farmers and ranchers and importing food from wherever they can find it the cheapest, despite worker and animal abuse and environmental degradation. We will lose our family farms and local food processors unless we are willing to support them."

After years of building up a ranch and feedlot, and now a farm-to-retail marketing business, Mike is still working every day on oversight and expansion of his various projects.

"Many weeks I'm driving a truck between Colorado and northwest Kansas. My grown son, Teegan, is involved in the family business, and he and his wife, Jenice, in turn have two sons, Wilson and Charlie, who are already showing an aptitude for building things. That's a long tradition in my family. I'm also a private pilot, which allows me to fly back and forth between my store in Colorado Springs and the ranch in northwest Kansas as needed."

As for his cooking skills, he admits that he does not fuss over complicated dishes, and not surprisingly, beef is a first choice.

"I cook very simply. I don't use recipes. Nothing to me is better than a good piece of meat cooked to medium rare and lightly seasoned. The most important thing is to know where that meat came from and that every step was taken to make it the best piece of meat it could be. Using high-quality cooking fats is also central to how I cook. Beef tallow, lard, butter, and olive oil are all less refined and less processed than corn, soybean, or canola oil, and much healthier."

Every time he sits down to a meal, Mike lives out his motto. He reflects on where the food came from and those who helped provide it. And he keeps working tirelessly to encourage others to join him in supporting local and regionally produced food. Having a connection to the people who raised it and understanding how it was produced is the basis for elevating eating to a moral act. Just as the meal of the Eucharist binds us all in the Church, we are also connected through the earthly food we eat.

Callicrate Beef Steak

In his description, note that Mike calls for Real Salt, a natural salt product that has not been processed, refined, nor bleached white. A market brand to look for is Redmond Real Salt, although other unrefined salt brands are available. He also advises that if beef tallow is not available, use a high-temperature fat or oil. But according to him, "beef tallow is the best."

Mike goes on to explain his "reverse sear method" of cooking beef.

"When considering the beef from high-quality, properly aged, well-raised, and processed cattle, there are many cuts, in addition to ribeye, strip, and tenderloin filet that can make a great steak. I prefer a steak at least 1 ½ inches thick, which usually means there is enough to share. The oven cast iron reverse sear method (sear the meat after oven cooking) works for any size cut of meat suitable for grilling. The cuts from the sirloin, like the coulotte or tri-tip steak, are often especially well marbled and make very nice single portion sizes while still maintaining a nice thickness."

Directions:

1. Allow the steak to come to room temperature prior to cooking. Season with Real Salt and coarse pepper.
2. Preheat the oven to 300 degrees F.
3. Use a good remote thermometer with a metal cable probe to monitor the internal temperature. Place the meat on a wire rack with the tip of the temperature probe inserted into the middle of the steak. Cook to 124 degrees.
4. Remove the steak and sear on both sides in beef tallow in a hot cast-iron skillet. Sear time will depend on the preferred doneness. Searing for 1 1/2 minutes on each side will make for a delicious medium rare. Place the steak on a warm plate and tent with tinfoil for 5 minutes.
5. Enjoy!

A Virginian Convert and Farmer

Jesse Straight

Out in the Storm

In 2007, Hurricane Sandy thrashed the northern part of the East Coast. When the storm hit, Jesse Straight realized he had a unique problem that most people were not dealing with: his turkeys were getting battered by the storm.

"When poultry feathers get wet, the bird loses all its protective heat. The wind and rain were coming in sideways, and the birds were keeling over from hypothermia and sinking in the mud."

For over five hours, he gathered up each of his turkeys, even if they were nearly dead, and put them into his barn.

"I was totally drenched. It was cold. It was windy. The birds were so distressed, and I felt badly because they were not protected."

Jesse Straight

Fortunately, his parents showed up and helped him gather the remaining birds, though he would end up losing nearly a quarter of the flock. It was a day he will never forget. "And I don't know if a hot shower ever felt better. I was cold down to the bones."

Walking the Path to Rome

Virginian Jesse Straight is charming, talented, and devoted to the farming life. He is also a staunch Catholic. But the pathway to his faith was not straight.

Growing up in Warrenton, Virginia, in an Evangelical home, Jesse has teased his parents that they raised him to be such a good Evangelical that he became Catholic. While he is thankful that his parents taught him true happiness is found in Christ, he was troubled by the disunity and the lack of firm doctrinal basis for the Protestant faith. He wanted a firmer foundation.

When he attended Eastern University in Philadelphia, he participated in the Great Books Program, which led him to an epiphany. "I realized Christianity is not just me and the Bible. It's a gift of the Church handing down the Scriptures and teachings and sacraments. These made me more appreciative of the historic Church."

Jesse transferred to the University of Virginia in Charlottesville, where he studied medicine and also theology. As a result, he shifted to a more traditionally oriented worship than he experienced during his Evangelical childhood.

"My wife and I went to an Anglo-Catholic Episcopal church for a while. But a new priest came in shortly after we began attending services there, and he was not as friendly to Anglo-Catholics. A group of our friends all discussed how unfortunate it was and we began to talk seriously about becoming Catholic."

A major influence on Jesse's faith at this time came from their neighbors in Charlottesville. "They were very devout, and their family life was compelling. They did all Catholic things together, like praying the Rosary and going on pilgrimages. I wanted those things for my family. The husband told me, 'Go to RCIA. Become Catholic.' Well, we did, and they were our sponsors as we entered the Church."

At the Easter Vigil in 2009, Jesse and his wife came into the Church, along with several other friends who joined them on their path to Rome over the next few years. One friend would even go on to become a Benedictine priest in Chicago.

Most fundamentally, Jesse says, they were convinced of the Catholic Church's argument for its own validity as the Church that Christ Himself founded. There was truly nothing else to believe if one embarked on an honest study of history. They also learned that Catholicism supported many other ideas and teachings dear to their hearts, such as nurturing a culture of life and a love of family, as well as how Catholic social teaching is supportive of an agrarian critique of modern life.

Whiffletree Farm

The Monday after they joined the Catholic Church, the young couple moved back to Warrenton to start a farm they would call Whiffletree.[5]

For a premed student who also studied theology, the choice of farming seemed odd to some. But Jesse explained that when trying to figure out his true life's goal, he was profoundly impressed by Wendell Berry's book *A World Lost.* The text is a critique of the transient nature of modern life that separates families, communities, and churches, offering a vision of the alternative good life that retains an integration of all the people, places, and parts of a person's life.

The book inspired him to focus on living this sort of life. Jesse decided that returning to Warrenton to work on a farm would bring him that integrated life he sought, where work, home, community, and yes, faith, would all fit together in perfect harmony, or at least as perfect as life can be in a fallen world.

The couple packed up their things and left Charlottesville to start their new farming life in rural Virginia. Since neither Jesse nor his wife had had any farming experience, they had to start this new life from scratch. He turned to other local farmers for advice, including Joel Salatin of Polyface Farm, someone who had become famous for his emphasis on sustainable farming.

Jesse decided to start farming on a small scale by just raising chickens for meat. The Straights had at least some experience with poultry back in Charlottesville, where they had raised laying hens in their backyard. The farm's initial batch included only 52 chickens, and the processed meat was just given away to family and friends. But as the couple gained confidence

---

[5] For more information, visit https://whiffletreefarmva.com.

in their work, they grew the batch to 150 chickens, and the numbers kept escalating.

Jesse then decided to add laying hens for eggs, and turkeys and livestock to his barns and pastures. At one point, he had 800 turkeys, 160 hogs, 70 cows, and more than 12,000 chickens.

As a successful farmer, as well as a clever businessman, he opened an on-site store that sells eggs, organic vegetables, local raw honey, grass-fed lamb, and other farm-based products. Customers can pick up their order directly from the store, or he and his staff deliver to various sites throughout Maryland, Washington, DC, and all throughout northern and central Virginia. He also sells to local restaurants, which accounts for about 60 percent of his business.

One of his proudest accomplishments, however, is establishing an intern program for aspiring farmers to learn sustainable farming practices. "It's a four-month program," Jesse says with a hint of pride. "They work with us and learn all about in-the-field farm operations, with opportunities to learn about the business side as well."

Not surprisingly, as Jesse summarizes his farming day, he and his staff are always busy. Each day begins at 5:30 a.m. with a review of what needs to be done that day. By 6:00 a.m., he is off for the fields to do his chores: feeding and watering hens and turkeys and moving them to fresh pastures or paddocks; giving baby chicks fresh bedding, clean water, and food; moving cattle to fresh pastures; and gathering eggs, among many other duties, some of which vary by season.

When these morning chores are finished, he and his farmhands gather for a quick breakfast before returning to their work, making deliveries, fixing the farm's infrastructure, running errands to pick up supplies, or driving livestock to the slaughterhouse. That usually extends through the majority of the day, until, before dinner, the crew checks in again on the cows, chickens, and turkeys, making sure there is plenty of water available for them.

"Maintaining good health for all our stock, land, and patrons is our fundamental goal. To accomplish this, we must approach the world as God has given it to us. In nature, animals are always on the move for quality food and a sanitary life, and as it turns out, all that is beneficial for the quality of the soil. The lands need grazing and fertilizing, and these were made to be in harmony with each other and most fitting to God's order."

Jesse adds that his kind of free-range farming means getting away from steel and concrete. "Most animals that Americans eat, whether they know it or not, are raised on concrete in confined barns. It lessens the vulnerability to weather and predators. Steel and concrete provide protection, but at what cost?"

Jesse prefers the "pasture model," meaning that such farmers want animals on pastured land. This comes with some kind of vulnerability to nature, but it's worth it in Jesse's opinion. It improves the health of the animal, which makes for better meat.

Food, of course, is a major part of a farmer's life, and for Jesse, he and his wife tag team the cooking—that is, one will cook while the other is taking care of the children.

"Liz and the kids do the brunt of cooking, but I make the weekend lunches. I am the waffle maker, and I make the bacon-fat popcorn. And during the week, I often make my own later breakfasts, which are more like large hodge-podge left-over dinners that happen to include eggs."

Jesse and his staff and family have created something of a rural paradise on their eighty acres. It's evident when you talk to him that he understands God has guided him to this life for a purpose. God has helped him understand the world and how he fits into it through farming.

"We want to follow God in the spirit of humility and practice of the Catholic faith. Our role is to love God and our neighbors and to thank God for all He has given us. I am grateful for all the people who buy our food—I feel a connection to them—and I am excited to see our land become more and more fertile."

Bacon Fat Popcorn

For Northern Virginians who can have access to Jesse Straight's farm products, he suggests for this recipe using the Whiffletree Farm bacon from pasture-raised, non-GMO, antibiotic-, chemical-, and nitrate-free pigs. Otherwise, one should pick up the best commercial product available, maybe from a local butcher.

He advises, "Be sure to use a large pot with a very flat bottom, otherwise the popcorn will not cook evenly."

THE FOLLOWING MAKES ABOUT TEN LARGE BOWLS OF POPCORN

Ingredients:

- 2 pounds bacon for 1 cup bacon fat
- About 2 cups organic corn kernels, or enough to line the bottom of cook pot 1 inch deep
- Celtic sea salt to taste

Directions:

1. Cook the bacon in a heavy skillet over medium heat. Remove the cooked bacon and reserve the fat. Do not discard any little pieces of cooked bacon.
2. Put 1 cup of bacon fat in a deep pot with a flat bottom. Line the bottom of the pot with corn kernels and spread them out so no kernel is on top of another. Turn the heat up to medium-high.
3. Once the kernels begin to pop and the pot is half full, keep the temperature at medium high, but stir the mixture with a wooden spoon. Look for any burning kernels. Remove the pot from the heat and keep stirring if you smell or see any bits of burning. Otherwise, keep stirring over medium–high heat until the popping gets about 5 seconds apart.
4. Remove from the heat and keep stirring for about 1 minute to prevent any burning. Season with the Celtic sea salt to taste and enjoy!

Fizzy Tea

For a drink to go with your Bacon Fat Popcorn, try Jesse's "fizzy tea."

1. Brew a large pot of your favorite herbal tea. "Ours is one of the teas concocted by Katherine Adam, a grower of tea leaves in Northern Virginia."
2. Sit it out to get to room temperature, then put it in fridge over night to chill. The following day, add in Soda Stream to carbonate. Enjoy your fizzy tea!

Loving
Her
Reality

Teri Guevremont

The Path to Reality

How many people could ever imagine farming on acreage in central Virginia that once hosted General George Washington's army?

Teri Guevremont

For more than 250 years, Reality Farm, nestled near the sloping lands of the Blue Ridge Mountains just a few hours from the DC metro area, has stunned visitors with its natural beauty, attracting city slickers and suburbanites looking for a country day trip. And it's not just the scenery they seek out; they can also shop for authentic farm goods at Reality Farm.

This is where Teri Guevremont lives and works the farming life. Such a life includes feeding a Brahman bull, delivering fresh goat's milk, and tending to an eclectic range of animals, including water buffalo, mini zebu (a mini Brahman), Chinese geese, goats, and chickens. Teri has lived this life for so long that it seems as if she always has been here, but it was a winding path that led her to Reality Farm, one that began south of the equator.

Born in Medellin, Colombia, the second largest city in the country and found in a central region of the Andres Mountains, Teri attended Catholic schools up until the twelfth grade, giving her a solid faith formation. She also had a devout family, particularly her grandmother, who was a prime example and a role model in her childhood. For that reason, Teri has always tried to live her faith and to grow closer to God, chiefly by attending daily Mass and by praying a daily Rosary.

Teri met her American husband when his military parents were stationed in Colombia. Years later while vacationing in Florida, they reconnected and were eventually married. Teri followed her husband, a marine himself, to various postings throughout the United States. Only when he retired did they settle in Great Falls, located in Northern Virginia. Life there began in the suburbs, but something began to stir in Teri.

Growing up in Medellin, Teri's family had a farm near their home that they would visit on weekends and holidays. Her experiences there inspired a love of farming that would call out to her shortly after their move to Great Falls. She suggested that they purchase a farm way out in central Virginia as a relaxing and pleasant vacation destination. It didn't hurt either that their daughter, Lizzie, had a dream of having her very own horse.

As fate played out, a family friend mentioned that a two-hundred-acre farm was for sale. Teri called the owner and set up a time for the couple to visit.

"We saw the farm, and it was like we were in another world. We loved everything about the land and the setting."

Though they would look elsewhere, nothing compared to Reality Farm, a name they kept after purchasing it since it had been called that for over two centuries.

"God pointed us in that direction, and it literally was our new reality."

After Teri and her husband moved to rural Virginia, they stocked their farmland with a herd of cows.

"I got a Jersey cow named Rosie. She gave us a lot of milk, about two gallons a day. I knew people nearby, and because we had all this milk we couldn't use, I contacted a foundation on the internet called Realmilk.com that helps farmers connect with consumers inter-ested in natural and locally produced foods. We also met numerous Catholic

families living in nearby Front Royal where Christendom College is, and they all wanted our raw milk."

A decade later, they acquired and were milking thirty-five to forty cows a day and were delivering milk five days a week all over Northern Virginia.

"I never in my life thought that I would be doing this, that we would be farming like this. Fortunately, my husband was on board, and we now have even opened a vineyard and a winery."

After attending a Weston Price Foundation conference, Terri and her husband began to focus on all-natural, all-organic goods.

"I was blown away by what the speaker told us about foods. The conference speaker talked about different diets and lots of supplements and the importance of good nutrition and wholesome milk. They offered milk samples, and I tried their raw milk. It was delicious. I was thinking that this is great, so how do I get raw milk to my customers?"

Before they had their own cows, the Guevremonts and a group of five other families began to drive out to a farm in Winchester, Virginia, to pick up the raw milk. After making it a part of their daily diet, she began to appreciate things she noticed about her family's health. They all switched to a natural diet, got rid of all processed foods, and made every meal from scratch.

The couple has also opened a farm store where customers can stop in to shop, or order online for delivery at specific locations in the area. Available products include cuts of beef, poultry, cheeses, local honey, and other dairy products. Potential farmers can select from among some of the various pure-bred breeds for sale, including Brahmas, Devons, Angus, Jersies, Holsteins, Guernseys, and Brown Swiss. They have also cross-bred these varieties to increase the overall vigor of the herd. According to their website, that includes Brahma with Jersey, Brown Swiss with Angus, and Devon with Jersey. Consumers can also purchase goat milk.[6]

Still more, Reality Farm has become a destination for picnics and day trips, and the couple has hosted parishioners from their nearby parish of St. Peter Catholic Church in Little Washington, Virginia.

---

[6] For more information, visit https://realityfarminc.com/store/.

Daily life has a balance of duties between the Guevremonts, their five children, and a few farmhands. Teri tends to the animals and makes local deliveries of dairy products, in addition to overseeing the creamery and making batches of goat's milk kefir. Her husband tends to the beef cattle and vineyards, performs routine repairs, and oversees the mending of fences and the winery, as well as the family kitchen.

"He does the cooking and meal preparations," Teri admits with a smile. "Some of our favorites are various cream of mushroom soups and the leek-and-potato soups, as well as soups with chicken broth and a lot of vegetables."

For her part, Teri makes plain and flavored yogurts and all the milk-based dishes, and she churns the cream to make butter. She also whips up smoothies with bananas or other fruits and mango lassi sweetened with stevia and spiced up with cinnamon.

Serving God and Neighbor through Our Labor

The most rewarding part of life on Reality Farm, according to Teri, is making a difference in the lives of the families they serve. "They are eating better. Our society is so far away from nature and from what God created for us. I have a passion for making the food that our ancestors enjoyed."

She thanks God daily for all she and her family have, and she knows that despite the exhaustion that comes from a life toiling on the farm, He is giving her the grace to keep going.

"My faith is part of my daily life. I get up early and do all my prayers, and I am a member of Opus Dei,[7] so I see my work as a part of my faith and my calling. The older I get, the more I see the teachings of Saint Josemaría Escrivá bearing fruit in my life. The labor we do can be an offering, a prayer, a way to serve God by serving your neighbor."

Despite the hectic pace of each day, Teri appreciates being so close to nature. "The sky, the stars . . . you can see God's hand in all these things, you can nurture a contemplative heart. In the city, you can miss that reality, that chance to find Him in the natural world. While contemplating nature, you can talk to God right there where you are, when you see what He has made, observing the change of seasons and everything else. I love what I do, and it has been a tremendous gift from God."

---

[7] Opus Dei is an institution of the Catholic Church. Their mission is to spread the message that every person is called to holiness through his work, family life, and ordinary events of each day, which are all opportunities for drawing closer to Christ and making Him known to others. It was founded in 1928 by Monsignor Josemaría Escrivá (now a canonized saint).

Potato-Leek Soup

This soup makes a great, healthy, and tasty addition to any meal. It can also be a stand-alone meal in itself.

SERVES 8

Ingredients:

- 2 pounds yellow gold potatoes
- 1 medium-sized sweet onion, peeled
- 1 head garlic
- 2 bunches leeks
- 4 tablespoons olive oil
- 7 cups chicken stock
- 1 cup heavy cream
- Salt and freshly ground black pepper to taste

Directions:

1. Peel and cut half of the potatoes into ½-inch cubes. Peel and cut the remaining potatoes into quarters. Dice the onion into small pieces. Peel and press all the garlic into a small container and set aside.

2. Wash the leeks and cut off the root base. Remove 2 to 3 of the outer leaves, those that are hard and wilted. Keep the crisp inner leaves and cut the entire bunch into approximately ¼-inch circles, starting at the bottom of the bunch and working towards the top. Discard the top deep green and typically tougher tips.

3. Add the olive oil to a large pot, add the chopped onion, and heat over medium heat. When the onions turn clear, add the chicken stock (see stock recipe). Add the quartered potatoes, and simmer until the potatoes are soft. Using a hand blender, purée the potatoes into the stock.

4. Add the leeks, pressed garlic, and diced potatoes to the stock and simmer until potatoes are done and leeks are soft. While the mixture is simmering, stir in the heavy cream and salt and pepper. (If desired, omit the pepper because of the relatively large amount of garlic.) Bring the mixture back to a simmer in less than 1 minute, remove from the heat and serve.

Chicken Stock

Teri explains how to make her lovely chicken stock.

"We keep several quarts of homemade chicken stock in the refrigerator as a base for all our soups and other recipes. We save all the bones from other chicken meals to add to the stocks if available. You can omit the salt, which is a preservative, if you use the stock within one day of preparation or freeze it to use later. The No-Salt Seasoning is sold at Costco, but if not available, add a pinch of the following: (organic if available) parsley, bay leaf, thyme, basil, oregano, savory, cumin, mustard seed, marjoram, coriander, cayenne pepper, and rosemary. We typically will make the stock once a week."

Ingredients:

- 1 whole chicken
- 1 head garlic
- 2 tablespoons salt
- 3 stalks celery, finely chopped
- 1 onion, peeled and diced
- 2 grated carrots
- 4 tablespoons Organic No-salt Seasoning

Directions:

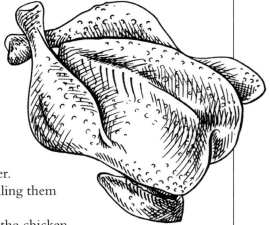

1. Place the chicken in a 6-quart pot and add all ingredients and enough water to within 1 inch of the rim, and bring to a boil.
2. Once the mixture starts to boil, cover and reduce the heat to low. Let it cook for at least 8 hours. It is best to place the pot on the stove in the evening, and let it simmer overnight. Take it off the heat in the morning.
3. When the contents have cooled, remove the chicken and strain the stock through a colander. Place strained stock into 2-quart mason jars filling them to the brim. Cap and refrigerate.
4. Remove the bones from the chicken and save the chicken for other meals, including soups, chicken salad, "arroz con pollo" (chicken and rice), and basically any dish that calls for a chopped bird.
5. Save the vegetable-and-spice mixture as a base for other soups and dishes. A family favorite is to add some leftover stock (usually several cups are left over after filling the jars) to the vegetables, plus a cup of quinoa. Bring the mixture to a boil and cook until the quinoa is tender.

A Professor
on the
Farm

John Cuddeback, PhD

The Burden of the Steward

Friendly, humble, and pious, farmer and professor Dr. John Cuddeback grows fruits and vegetables on his family's homestead in the Shenandoah Valley. He also raises many different kinds of animals, which he admits brings a mental and emotional burden down upon him when he is faced with slaughtering one for his family. Imagine the tension and anguish of killing an animal he has raised since birth.

"The animal trusts me, which makes it harder emotionally to kill it. But then again, this makes it better for the animal,

John Cuddeback, PhD

because I will be able to kill it without its knowing what is coming. It's always hard. But if we're going to receive the gift of meat, an animal must die. I want it to die as well as we can reasonably hope for, and it should be put to good use. This is our obligation as God's stewards."

Professor and Farmer

Noted for his outstanding stance on all things Catholic, Dr. John Cuddeback is a philosophy professor at Christendom College in Front Royal, Virginia.

"I have been searching for truth and wisdom for many years because I love them so much. I love having the opportunity to help others in their pursuit of wisdom. A liberal arts education is more and more important these days as a way of forming youth for a more fully human life, and for giving them the

principles to navigate the troubled waters of today. I love philosophy, and I'm honored to have been trying to share it with others for thirty years."

Besides teaching, Dr. Cuddeback is also a frequent speaker/presenter for the Institute of Catholic Culture, also headquartered in Front Royal. But perhaps his most noteworthy efforts, surely those closest to his heart, involve his work on his family homestead ("mini farm"). It is on this peaceful slice of earth that he devotes his time to food, family, and faith.

A native of Columbia, Maryland, and raised in an ardent Catholic family, Dr. Cuddeback not only learned about his faith early on but also watched and learned about farming from his father.

"My father was always interested in growing things. We had a family garden from my earliest days. He passed on his love of these things to me. Even as a youngster, I yearned to have a deeper connection to the land and to an established semi-rural community. A garden is a significant way of cultivating the earth. In gardening, most of us can have the opportunity to take care of the soil, to enjoy the earth's bounty, and to improve the soil to promote better crops. For me, gardening and other such homesteading projects are an effort to reconnect not only with the earth but with myself and with others."

Dr. Cuddeback admits that he had to learn the craft of farming slowly.

"Farming requires a prudential judgment of what I and my family can do," he explains. "We have about ten acres of open land and forty of woods, but we really only use several acres of each for agricultural purposes. We also find in it a lesson that following nature's lead in our farming practices redounds to the benefit of all involved—land, plants, animals, and especially, humans."

He and his wife, Sofia, have named their homestead Fair Knowe, after a Scottish cottage in a Sir Walter Scott novel.

But now, with years of experience behind him, he raises assorted crops, such as lettuce, chard, squash, cucumbers, and fruits such as figs, blueberries, and blackberries. He also harvests honey from their own beehives and raises several types of animals.

"We raise goats for meat and chickens for eggs. Almost all of what we raise is for the use of family and friends. There is a great economic benefit for our household, though we actually sell very little of what we produce. We use organic and sustainable methods—with somewhat variable success—and try to follow the maxim to leave the land a better place than we found it."

He has also raised a cow or two, and his farm is home to heritage pigs, which he raises and fattens on acorns. It is this diet he provides for his pigs that led to his blog and website, originally named "Bacon from Acorns." He finds the bacon his pigs provide to be an amazing sign of God's loving generosity in the natural world. Abundant acorns make the meat and lard of pigs to be not only more flavorful but also more nourishing.

Dr. Cuddeback's blog has grown into a central and defining feature of his professional life. As a result, he started offering a "Wednesday Quote"—a quotation from some great thinker, often ancient, accompanied by a brief reflection on a topic pertaining to anything from the heights of philosophy to gardening tips or culture in the home. Hence his blog and his website are now called Lifecraft.[8]

Still doing Wednesday Quotes, Dr. Cuddeback expanded the blog to include other resources, especially the online course "Man of the Household." The content of his work remains focused around basic themes of living the good life in the home and close to the land.

Home gardening, or farming, is Cuddeback's main approach to helping others see how cultivating the earth provides countless benefits.

"Sirach 7:15 says: 'Do not hate toilsome labor, or farm work, which were created by the Most High.' I am convinced that cultivating the earth is a unique gift from the Lord that tends to develop good moral dispositions and wisdom in those who do it well."

[8] See https://life-craft.org/.

Coming Together Over Food

While tending the earth as a farmer, Dr. Cuddeback strives to tend to his soul through his love of the Catholic Church.

"I am a lay Third Order Dominican. It's a vocation that fits well with my vocation to be a teacher since the Dominicans are known as teachers. I also feel a deep connection with the Benedictine tradition, and I enjoy going on retreat at Clear Creek Abbey, a monastery of Benedictine monks in eastern Oklahoma. The rhythm of their life is connected to the rhythm of the natural world, and this is something we all can try to do in our own lives. In an age of separation, division, and isolation, living close to the land is a powerful force for uniting people and households with one another and with the gift of God's creation."

He continues, "I love the breviary, and praying the hours of the Divine Office when I can. This is a beautiful way to bring praise to God and incorporate the rhythm of the liturgical calendar into our daily lives. I strive to live in the presence and knowledge of God's Holy Word in Scripture. I should do a much better job of it, but I strive to remember that man does not live on bread alone, but on every word that comes forth from the mouth of God."

He and his wife—who he admits is in charge of the kitchen despite his love of cooking—bring the family together by making cooking a family affair.

"Cooking with home-produced products adds a special joy and satisfaction to work in the kitchen. It's also a good reminder of God's generosity and His desire to be intimately involved in our home life."

For the Cuddebacks, as it is for most families, food is more about being together than it is about preserving human life.

"We can imagine technology producing a pill that could fulfill all our nutritional needs. But we would reject it out of hand. Food is about so much more than our nutritional needs."

As for what they eat, Dr. Cuddeback says he keeps things simple, leaving the more complicated dishes to his wife and children.

"My wife has mentored the children through the years, usually beginning in their teens. I am very grateful that she is passing on this powerful and beautiful art so important in home-making. I do make simple dishes, usually focused on foods we have grown or raised."

His simple offerings include the salads made with fresh greens from his garden. These include lettuces of many different varieties spiced up with arugula.

"Depending on the season, we can add tomatoes, cucumbers, and onions, as well as other young greens such as chard or beet greens. Sofia has taught me to make simple salad dressings of oil and vinegar with mustard and herbs. We really prefer our home dressings to the overly sweet store-bought dressings."

Cuddeback also prepares sides of bacon after the pigs are slaughtered, smoking the sides, then cutting and freezing them. He said he has no special recipe for the bacon, but acorn-fattened bacon that is salted and then smoked with the family's home-cut hickory wood is like magic.

"For Sunday brunch, I'm the bacon man, as well as the fried eggs-to-order man. In season, we love having our home-grown eggs. But whatever we have, it's all about coming together and giving thanks to God."

Easy Butternut Squash Soup

The good professor has chosen to share one of his own garden-inspired recipes with us, one that is a good way to use fall produce. One can follow the ingredients and directions, or, he suggests an extra possibility.

"Put the seeds on the tray next to the squash in the oven, with salt, pepper, and possibly curry (we love the curry). Roast the seeds for about the first 20 minutes of the hour of baking and then remove them from the oven, putting the squash back in to complete the hour. Roasted seeds are delicious as a snack or can be added to the soup when served. Enjoy!"

SERVES 4 TO 6

Ingredients:

- 1 or 2 butternut squash
- ½ to 1 stick unsalted butter
- Salt to taste
- Sprinkling of nutmeg

Directions:

1. Cut the squash in half, and scoop out the seed pods, saving the seeds.
2. Preheat the oven to 350 degrees. Bake squash halves face down on a baking tray for about an hour—basically until they can be easily scooped out of the skin.
3. In a saucepan, heat the butter over medium heat until it browns.
4. Add the scooped-out squash to the saucepan, briefly sautéing the squash. Then add water to cover the squash, according to how thick you want the soup.
5. Bring the soup to a boil. It is now ready. Prior to serving, blend either with a hand wand or in a large blender. (We prefer the hand wand.) Salt to taste. Try sprinkling some nutmeg when served.

Priests

A Chef
with a
Collar

Fr. John McNamara

Before the Seminary Came the Kitchen

Fr. John McNamara

Noted for his friendly greetings and cheerful conversations with parishioners, Fr. John McNamara has developed a following in his parish. A native of Mundelein, Illinois, and later of Arlington Heights, he currently (2022) serves as pastor at St. Catherine of Siena in West Dundee, Illinois, and at St. Mary's in Gilberts, Illinois. Father McNamara remembers well his devout Catholic family. They attended Mass regularly and prayed before meals, and his parents' faith inspired him to be true to Catholicism. All that likely played a strong influence in his eventual journey to the priesthood.

But God had other plans for him first, plans that led him into the kitchen to become a chef. As a child, his passion for cooking came from the family parties for which both his grandmother and aunts cooked.

"I always hung out in the kitchen, and I learned from them. I would help and I learned their cooking tricks."

In high school, he also worked for Pizza Hut and an ice cream and burger shop called Cock Robin. These jobs in the food industry, and a home economics class he enjoyed in school, led him to Harper College, a community college in Palatine, Illinois, where he got a degree in hospitality.

"I wanted to learn about the restaurant industry and about hotel management, and about the art of professional cooking. I received an internship with Elegante Cuisine in the suburbs of Chicago. I learned a ton about food there. They did catering for business dining events, and we would bring in the staff. I mainly worked as a prep cook. We also did parties for onsite events and private dinners where I would cook and serve in people's homes."

While with Elegante Cuisine, he was introduced to catering for the entertainment world and the musicians who came into town to perform.

After that, Father McNamara would join Aramark, a customer-service company in Chicago specializing in food, facilities, and uniforms, helping to oversee catering and cooking for local companies.

"I worked there from about 2000 to 2007. I began as a chef for Baxter Healthcare's headquarters with a kitchen of about twenty cooks. We served breakfast, lunch, and dinner, and we were cooking for about 1,500 people a day. I thought that was a lot, until I went to Kraft General Foods and ran a kitchen that fed 2,000 people a day! Someone would be making Italian food, some Chinese food, some running the grill, some making salads, and others focused on comfort foods, all made to order. We would also manage the daily catering orders throughout the company's building."

Cooking On the Road

From there, a chance reunion with one of the owners of Elegante Cuisine changed his course yet again.

"I got a call from my previous boss at Elegante to do catering for a Christmas party for a corporate executive. While I was at the party, my friend talked to me about a call he received from the country band Rascal Flatts. They wanted him to provide food service for the band and crew while on tour. I prayed about it and decided it was a good opportunity. I took the job, went to work, and traveled the country. Their semi-truck was transformed into a mobile kitchen. That quickly expanded as we got a call from Kenny Chesney's producer. I went on tour with them for the next seven months. That was a huge operation. We traveled in a tour bus and would wake up at 5:00 a.m. to start our day. We provided breakfast, lunch, and dinner for the crew and band, which amounted to hundreds of people."

"Our show day would typically wind down around 10:00 p.m., at which time we would load the truck and head to the next town to set up. A few hours of bumpy sleep in the bus would suffice until that alarm got us up for the next day's work. We went to every state in the continental United States and to Canada. It was a lot of work. The food industry is tough to begin with, but when it's taken on the road, there are that many more challenges."

Answering the Call

Father McNamara soon realized he was too worn out to keep up the pace this job required. He was also troubled by the way this lifestyle pulled him away from his faith. He rarely went to Mass and admits he lived a wild life while on the road.

"I knew I had to make a change. I felt the Holy Spirit touching my heart, prompting me back to my faith. I went to confession and one thing led to the next, and I returned home. It was at this time that I began to discover my call to the priesthood."

Father McNamara took a job running a small Italian restaurant in Wisconsin, during which time the Holy Spirit continued to work on him.

"God was calling me out of the food service industry. I could feel it. There was a chapel near where I worked, and I started going several times a week asking the Lord what I should do with my life. I discerned that God was calling me to be a priest. I came back to Chicago and spoke to a spiritual director and a vocation director. After a couple months, I went to Medjugore and had a great experience there. It was very sacramental, with confession, adoration, and Mass."

Fortunately, his business partner understood the change taking place, and Father McNamara had the support of his parents and family. He applied to the Diocese of Rockford Illinois, was accepted, and attended Holy Apostles Seminary in Cromwell, Connecticut, where he got a Master's in Theology. He was ordained a priest in 2015.

Cooking with a Collar On

And as for cooking?

"It's still a passion of mine. I still do private events for parishioners, or I cook for the kids in the school."

Father McNamara also regularly cooks for other priests in the rectory, and for parish events, such as for the Knights of Columbus, for whom he is the chaplain.

"For the Knights, we held a few pasta and homemade meatballs-and-tomato sauce dinners. We would make about five or six hundred meatballs. These were for a fundraiser, and it would always go over well."

His other popular dishes include pretzels, pizzas, crêpes, ice cream, and similar offerings. For parish picnics, he serves up traditional hot dogs, burgers, and brats along with his brother knights.

As he gets shuffled from parish to parish (for such is the life of a diocesan priest), he sees food as a means to bond with his new parish family.

"I want to invite parish families over to the rectory to cook for them, and that way I get to know them better. And I would also like to have more fundraisers that revolve around cooking."

Considering his extensive cooking career, there are dozens, maybe even hundreds, of recipes that he loves. But he narrows his list of favorites down to a variety of Italian foods, dishes he learned during his time in Wisconsin at the Italian restaurant. He also enjoys preparing dishes with fresh seafood.

"I have worked with lots of different seafoods, such as fresh lobster on the East Coast and sea bass and halibut on the West Coast. It's always fun to come up with creative seafood dishes."

But, he adds, "I have been so far removed from the industry and new ingredients and new styles. I have not tuned into them, so I am a pretty standard cook, using recipes and styles of cooking that are mostly traditional."

When asked if he misses his former career, Father McNamara smiles but shakes his head.

"I've never felt a longing to go back to it. My life now is so Catholic and Eucharistic. I still have a passion to cook and eat, but I do not want to go back to the food industry."

Even so, he believes that those years in the food industry taught him valuable lessons.

"I'm grateful for all the experiences, and I truly believe that it all prepared me more deeply for my relationship with the Lord and serving others. The food service industry helped me to really learn about humanity. It gave me a deeper appreciation of where humanity struggles and has this deep hunger for the infinite. It became very clear that God is the ultimate fulfillment of everyone's heart. I want to do my best in bringing the Lord to people."

Now a priest for six years (as of June 2021), he reflects, "I'm no longer feeding bellies; I'm feeding souls. I'm helping people on their spiritual journeys and having them focus on what is most important. It has been fantastic to proclaim the Gospel, and it has all helped me grow closer to Our Lord through prayer, relationships with the community, and the ministry."

Penne Augustino

Father McNamara claims this pasta dish was a customer favorite at Auggies, the northern Wisconsin restaurant at which he worked. The tomato filets are from fresh, vine-ripened tomatoes that have been peeled and packed in their own juice. As a substitute, you can use canned whole peeled tomatoes that you then chop. This sauce works well in other pasta dishes too. Save and refrigerate or freeze the extra sauce. For a little extra spiritual punch in the recipe, follow in Father McNamara's footsteps: "I always used blessed salt ordered from the local priest."

Tomato Pomadoro Sauce

Ingredients:

- 2 to 3 tablespoons olive oil
- 2 to 3 tablespoons minced fresh garlic
- 1 #10 can 74/40 tomato filets, or canned whole peeled tomatoes, chopped
- 1 tablespoon kosher salt and freshly ground black pepper
- 1 generous handful chopped fresh basil
- ¼ cup chopped fresh Italian parsley
- 1 to 2 tablespoons sugar

Directions:

1. In a large saucepan over medium heat, add the olive oil and minced garlic, and cook, stirring, until the garlic turns a pale gold.
2. Add the tomatoes, and season with salt and pepper.
3. Reduce the heat to low and cook for about 1 hour. Stir in the chopped basil, chopped parsley, and the sugar, and season to taste.

Augustino

SERVES 2

Ingredients:

- Tomato pomadoro sauce
- ½ pound penne pasta
- 2 tablespoons olive oil
- Six 1-ounce patties of ground Italian sausage
- 10 pitted Kalamata olives
- Minced garlic to taste
- ¼ cup red wine
- Bleu cheese crumbles or shaved Pecorino Romano cheese
- Chopped fresh basil

Directions:

1. When the sauce is cooked, put on a pot of salted water over medium heat. When the water is at a rolling boil, add the penne and cook until tender. Remove from the heat.
2. In a large saucepan over medium–high heat, add the olive oil and sausage patties. Brown the patties on each side, and when almost fully cooked, add the Kalamata olives and the minced garlic.
3. When the garlic turns golden, add the red wine and 8 ounces of the Pomodoro sauce.
4. Reduce the heat to low for about 3 minutes, then add the cooked pasta plus a splash of pasta water.
5. Toss the pasta with the sauce and serve in a deep pasta bowl. Garnish with the cheese of choice and a sprinkling of chopped basil.
6. Enjoy!

The Chef Priest

Fr. Leo Patalinghug

Finding God between the Pots and Pans

If you are food savvy, watch the Food Network, or are a Catholic who tunes into EWTN, you most likely know the name of Fr. Leo Patalinghug. This renowned "cooking priest" specializes in connecting food with faith. To spread that message, he travels relentlessly from towns and world-wide, giving talks and cooking demonstrations. His chief goal is not to share recipes but to teach about God's love, referring to the teachings of Saint Teresa of Avila, whose lesson was that finding God meant looking "between the pots and pans."

Fr. Leo Patalinghug

New Communities and Good Food

Father Leo's parents moved to the Baltimore area from the Philippines when he was just a toddler. Though both his parents were Catholic, his father converted from the Baptist faith through his mother's example.

His parents quickly became popular in their new community because of their sense of hospitality.

"They celebrated regularly," Father recalls. "They had friends over every weekend, and people visiting helped her in the kitchen all the time. That had an influence on their hospitality, and I saw who my parents welcomed. My dad was a doctor and helped many Filipinos from house to house."

His mother's Filipino dishes were incredibly flavorful, so tasty, in fact, that it made Father a few friends.

"I think the only reason I had any friends is because kids from the neighborhood would come over to eat my mother's cooking," he jokes.

"And parents would come as well. Her ability to touch hearts and minds through the stomach had a great influence. I think the reason my family had so many friends was because my mother cooked so well. Thankfully, she taught me a lot of the basics that I still remember to this day."

Answering the Call

As a youngster, Father Leo went to Saint Rose of Lima church in Baltimore only to please his parents, who wanted him to learn to be kind to others. One Sunday, he attended Mass on his own, and a visiting missionary priest came up to him after Mass. He invited the young boy to talk with him about missions and helped him to understand their importance. Subsequently, he went on a pilgrimage to Medjugorje, a life-changing trip, when he was nineteen years old.

"I experienced a great conversion on the pilgrimage to Medjugorje, especially on my Sunday there at the church. I want people to see themselves as pilgrims and to be shepherded out of their comfort zone, where they can discover the beauty that the Catholic Church has brought to the world."

As a junior at the University of Maryland in Baltimore, he began to feel a call to the priesthood. Nevertheless, he continued on with his studies, receiving degrees in political science and journalism. It wasn't until a year later that he called the vocations office in Baltimore.

Why did he choose the priesthood?

"I believe God called me to that ministry. The parish mission preacher had a huge influence on me. And some of the priests invigorated my soul to be a priest, a mission preacher, trying to hook people in with food—people are hungry spiritually and physically. I was trying to search out the truth by becoming a youth minister. And suddenly I felt a draw to the priesthood, this after many years of not caring about Mass. I had once been an eye-rolling teen. Who would have thought I'd become a priest?"

He said his parents were shocked when he told them of his decision, but they were incredibly supportive.

"My mother had been praying that one of her children would come into the ministry. I am blessed because my parents are saints."

Grace before Meals

Later, as a seminarian in Rome, Father Leo noted that all the seminarians were required to share meals in the community.

"I was immersed in Italian culture, long meals, and the churches in Rome. Why is Rome most traveled to? Because of faith and food!"

After becoming a deacon, he attended a retreat at the Pontifical North American College in Rome. While there, a clinical psychologist spoke to the attendees and said something that resonated with Father Leo.

"During a silent meal, she reflected on where food comes from. Some of us thought that was a little hokey. But I started getting emotional and kept thinking of our farmers, our servers, our chefs, our ancestors. If you keep going back, you get to our heavenly Father as the provider. I experienced a sacramental moment of God's embrace, an internal embrace. It came through food. When it gets down to it, food is the primary thing that people are working for, whether migrants or anyone else. Look at the world wars. What people are fighting for is a loaf of bread. That thought stayed with me and got me closer to the Eucharist and to becoming a chef."

In fact, just before the seminarians were ordained, Father Leo decided to choose Jesus's passage, "'Do you love me?' And He said, 'Feed my sheep.'" And so this was how Father Leo would spend his life, feeding Christ's flock.

During his first years as a parish priest at St. John's Catholic Church in Westminster, Maryland, Father Leo often joined parishioners for dinner. On one occasion, he told the family that he would come cook for them instead of the other way around. He was trying to answer Christ's call to serve rather than be served.

Later, while on retreat in France, the terrorist attacks of 9/11 took place. All flights were cancelled and they were stranded there. The priests extended their retreat and spent time in prayer for the victims of the attacks and for peace. Father Leo cooked for everyone, much to their enjoyment, so much so that they suggested he become a professional "chef/priest" with his very own cooking show. This would lead to his *Grace Before Meals* cookbook, as well as the wider Grace Before Meals movement, which strives to bring families back to the dinner table—away from work, school, TV, games—to share a delicious meal together, communicate, and love one another and be nourished in body, mind, and soul.

"Grace Before Meals is centered on one fundamental concept: the simple act of creating and sharing a meal can strengthen all kinds of relationships. Research has been done to show that the family that eats (and prays) together will stay together, so it is our mission to give families the tools they need to come together at dinnertime and be nourished in all areas of life. Luckily, these 'tools' are simply delicious and easy-to-make recipes, ideas for talking together, and prayers to bring God to the table."

But that would all come down the road for Father Leo. First, he knew he needed to hone his cooking skills. He took courses with a chef from Cordon Bleu in Perugia, Italy, and received a cooking certificate.

"I met with the chef and we became friends. He taught me a lot. I am still connected to my chef friends."

Father Leo has made friends with chefs all over the world. With each of them, he asks, "How do you practice what you are taught?"

"I learn from all of them. Everywhere I go, I learn about that cuisine,

whether it is Asian, European, Latino, and even parts of America. I become a disciple to that food and to those people."

When the Food Network came out, he was of course an avid follower, practicing with the dishes he would watch being prepared on the various shows.

Then came the moment that introduced Father Leo onto the national scene. He received an invitation to compete in a cooking competition at Mount St. Mary University in Emmitsburg, Maryland. When he showed up, he discovered the competition was a surprise chance to compete on the Food Network's "Throwdown! With Bobby Flay." Bobby Flay himself was there! The competition—"Steak Fajita Throwdown"—pitted him against several other talented chefs, but the judges selected Father Leo's offering because of the quality of the steak's sauce and the way the meat was seared. After the show wrapped, Father Leo gathered with family and friends in Baltimore's Little Italy, where they enjoyed seeing him win the competition.

Since that time, Father Leo has spent his time and energy—and cooking skills—spreading the word of God through his cooking. For several years, he has hosted his own TV program on EWTN called "Savoring our Faith." As he cooks, he often interviews guests about their faith. But his vocations don't end there. He has also established his own website called Plating Grace;[9] he has created a docuseries called "Feeding the Flock"; he records a podcast on Apple called "Shoot the Shiitake with Father Leo"; and he leads three pilgrimages a year to the faith-and-food capitals of Spain, Italy, and the Holy Land. He also works with Chefs for Peace from many other ethnic groups.[10]

As he travels around the world to give talks and cooking demonstrations, he notes, "Part of my mission is to feed people without the pressure to convert. Like Mother Teresa and Saint Paul, I evangelize, not proselytize. I was once in a city, Nablus, near the Holy Land. I asked if we could have Palestinians and Jews together to cook. I aim to bring people together through food. If I give everyone the same ingredients to make hummus, I would like each person to share it with each other and it would make us eat together."

He added that that has not happened yet, but he is hoping it will one day.

It is estimated that Father Leo speaks to about fifty thousand people a year, although he will never forget that night on the Food Network with Bobby Flay when two million viewers looked on. Afterwards, he received a note from a viewer thanking him, noting that she had walked away from her Catholic faith thirty years before. She was inspired to go to confession and to attend Mass again. Even if just this one soul was touched, all of Father Leo's hard work was worth it.

---

[9] Visit https://platinggrace.com.
[10] Father Leo has also written four books: *Saving the Family: The Transformative Power of Sharing Meals with People You Love*; *Epic Food Fight: A Bite-Sized History of Salvation*; *Grace Before Meals: Recipes and Inspiration for Family Meals and Family Life: A Cookbook*; and *Spicing up Married Life Satisfying Couples' Hunger for True Love*. He is currently working on two more books on how to keep college kids faithful and how to feed the flock without boring them.

Arroz Caldo

Father Leo tells us, "This traditional Filipino dish—translated as a savory 'hot rice soup'— is a basic chicken and rice soup but flavored with Asian ingredients, such as ginger, garlic, and aromatics like 'fish sauce' or soy sauce. It is a homey comfort food and eaten anytime during the early mornings or very late at night. It's a portable and shareable dish, often times served after the evening Masses prior to Christmas."

SERVES 4

Ingredients:

- 2 boneless chicken breasts, cut into ½-inch cubes
- 2 teaspoons salt and pepper, (plus more to taste)
- 1 tablespoon vegetable oil
- 1 medium-sized white onion, peeled and finely chopped
- 2 garlic cloves, peeled and minced
- 1 tablespoon grated fresh ginger
- 1 cup uncooked white rice (jasmine or long grain)
- 7 to 10 cups chicken broth, simmering
- 3 pinches red pepper flakes (optional)
- 1 tablespoon of "fish sauce" or soy sauce as an alternative
- Tabasco sauce, optional
- 2 scallions, minced, for garnish

Directions:

1. Season the chicken cubes with 2 teaspoons salt and black pepper; mix together and set aside.
2. Heat the oil in a large saucepan or pot over medium heat. Add the onion, garlic, and ginger, and sauté until the onions are translucent, approximately 1 minute.
3. Immediately add the chicken and brown on all sides. Add the rice to the mixture and cook, stirring until the rice becomes slightly translucent, approximately 1 to 2 minutes.
4. Add the hot chicken broth 1 cup at a time, stirring so that the rice becomes creamy. This usually takes about 2 to 3 minutes. Continue to add the broth and continue to stir. Make sure the rice is always covered with 1/2 inch of broth.
5. Add the red pepper flakes and fish sauce. Allow the broth to come to a light boil, cooking the rice.
6. When the rice is soft, the soup is finished. The soup is generally served thick, almost like porridge, but it should also have some broth as well, like a traditional chicken and rice soup. To thin it out, just add 1 or 2 cups of borth and be sure to season accordingly. Serve with a few splashes of Tabasco sauce, if desired, and a sprinkle of scallions for garnish and extra flavoring.

A Bayou
Father
and Cook

Fr. Bill John Melançon

Kitchen Mishaps

Kitchen memories can last for years, and as Fr. Bill John Melançon points out, those memories can be fond ones, or ones of mishaps.

Fr. Bill John Melançon

"In the pantry and cabinets, one can mistake salt for sugar or vanilla extract for any other dark liquid in a bottle. Things spill and things fall. One day, I was cooking fresh bread rolls for a church gathering, over two hundred rolls made from scratch. Just let the yeast rise, make the dough, and let it rise again. Most of the rolls were made when some staff workers came over to help. Reluctantly, I allowed them. I needed a break! I walked out of the kitchen just as the last couple dozen rolls were placed in the oven. 'You can take them out in fifteen to twenty minutes,' I told them. When I was walking back, I heard a crash! As they were taking the rolls out of the oven, they missed placing the pans on the large island. There were rolls all over the place! And yes, the rolls rolled! The staff members looked a little frightened awaiting my reaction."

After ensuring no one was burned or otherwise hurt, Father Bill began to laugh. "This is the last time I'll let someone help me!"

Everyone chuckled and all was well, for there were still plenty of rolls to go around.

A Bayou Priest

Fr. Bill John Melançon, pastor at St. Rita Catholic Church in Catahoula, Louisiana, was born in Saint Martinville and grew up in the nearby village of Loreauville. After stints in various places, he has returned close to home and is delighted to serve in this small parish after a lengthy pastoral career. And there is little doubt his parishioners are glad to have him, for among his other cheerful attributes, Father Bill is a talented cook.

He attributes his culinary skills to his mother and to growing up in an area of Louisiana where cooking and food are all part of everyday life. His parents were sugarcane sharecroppers, which also influenced him.

"I learned in Louisiana we liked to eat and to spend time with each other. It is a community built around food. Dining together is a great opportunity for good outreach among Catholics and others in our community."

Raised in a densely Catholic area of Louisiana by devout parents, Father Bill knew even at the age of six that he wanted to become a priest. He fell in love with God early in life and wanted to be like the priests he witnessed at the altar. But his route to priesthood had a few unexpected twists and turns.

After attending a secular college in Lafayette, he entered St. Joseph Seminary College in Covington, Louisiana. He then moved to Washington, DC to study at the Catholic University of America, where he took classes in theology as a seminarian. But he decided to leave the seminary and took several jobs thereafter: as a director of religious education at Saint Bernadette's in Bayou Vista, Louisiana; as a salesman of home kitchen products; and then as an elementary Catholic school teacher at Saint Joseph Elementary School in Jeanerette, Louisiana.

In 1989, Father Bill entered the Discalced Carmelite Order as a postulant for formation in Washington, DC. He then entered the novitiate in Holy Hill, Wisconsin. Periodically, he was asked to cook in the monastery, and he baked cinnamon rolls and cookies and sold them for fundraisers. In 1991, upon his return as a student friar some months later to Washington, Father Bill's winding path took yet another turn. He woke up one spring morning realizing he needed to return to Louisiana.

His diocesan bishop accepted his return and sent him to Mount St. Mary's University in Emmitsburg, Maryland to complete his theology and pastoral studies. He stayed for one year, travelling to classes at the Catholic University of America. In May of 1993, he was ordained a transitional deacon at the Shrine of Saint Elizabeth Ann Seton in Emmitsburg, and in the fall, he was ordained a Roman Catholic priest for the Diocese of Lafayette.

Life in the Kitchen

Upon his return to Louisiana, Father Bill was assigned as parochial vicar to St. Genevieve Catholic Church in Lafayette. This is where his status as a local cooking and baking superstar began.

"I would make chocolate chip cookies the size of pizzas," he recalls, laughing. "We had an elementary and a high school, and I would bring the cookies to the faculty of both schools."

His next assignment was to the Sacred Heart of Jesus Church in Baldwin, Louisiana. There, he participated in an annual church fundraising event called the Garfish Festival, at which he would cook red beans and rice or white beans and rice to complement the garfish and fried alligator tails. (Garfish have a long, slender body with sparkling scales and may grow up to ten feet long. It is also known as "alligator gar" because of its sharp teeth, but it has no relation to alligators.)

"The garfish eggs are like caviar and are called 'gold' because the eggs are golden in color. People wanted to buy garfish balls (boulets) because they are like crab cakes. These were deep-fried and were very good! When we had big events, I would also cook a dessert."

Father attributes his comfort in the kitchen to his mother's passion for cooking. Her influence is why he loves to make gumbo and jambalaya and other traditional bayou dishes. As a youth, no matter where he went in Louisiana, he always looked forward to coming home and watching his mother cook.

"I was not allowed in the kitchen to help her until I was a teenager because when I was very young, I got in her way," Father Bill admits. "When I was old enough, I began to help, and I joined the local 4-H Club and learned to bake goods and enter them into contests. That's when the fad of pizzas started, and I learned how to make them. Dad loved my pizzas!"

After these foundational childhood experiences, his bond with food was strengthened when he went to the Discalced Carmelite Monastery at Holy Hill, where his religious brothers asked him to whip up Louisianan dishes, like the gumbos he knew so well. He was also asked to fix a dinner for parish volunteers where he would be in charge of cooking for over seventy people.

"The recipe was for confetti chicken, and I was cooking in quantity. I would be preparing the whole meal, from appetizers to desserts. Thankfully, everyone loved the food."

He remembers how at the monastery how each brother was asked to cook once a month, but for him, it became close to once a week.

"That was fine by me, because then I did not have to clean the pots and pans—thus went the separation of duties! We were feeding about twenty people. On Sunday evenings, we would cook hot dogs and other easy dishes, and we were really relaxed. Once I made sweet-and-sour pork, and that was also relatively easy. I made my own starter for sourdough bread, and so we had fresh bread often. That's when my cooking life really took off."

As Father reflects on his cooking at different parishes, his time at St. Peter's Roman Catholic Church in Carencro, Louisiana sticks out.

"Besides cooking for people in the office, I started a program called Fasting with Father. We would fast all day, then after Mass and Stations of the Cross in the evening, I would prepare a simple meal of soup and bread for everyone. The parishioners all seemed to love it, so I kept it going until, eventually, they took over, but I would then make some desserts. It was a lovely way to turn a beneficial spiritual practice like fasting into a community event where we could all support each other."

But cooking activities around the parish grounds didn't stop there for Father Bill.

"Later, at the school, twice they auctioned off a seven-course meal for eight people, and it made a good deal of money. We cooked the seven-course meals in the parish hall, and one time we decorated the hall to show off our meals from around the world. We started in Cajun Land, and in true culinary fashion, travelled to Italy, France, Australia, and back to Louisiana. The faculty were my sous chefs, and guests were waited on by eighth graders. We did it for two years and brought in a lot of money. As it turned out, people asked me to come to their home and wanted to know what I would cook for them. They said they would buy the ingredients and we would cook jambalayas and gumbos."

At his next parish, he would bake bread for events and prepare Seder meals during Holy Week. For the St. Joseph's Altar at that church, he prepared over five hundred cookies, including his fig cookies for which he is so famous. At another parish, he prepared jambalayas, chicken fricassee, and gumbos for the volunteers, and he would always put out a dessert. At nearly all the parishes Father Bill has been stationed, there have been food festivals, including alligator and crawfish festivals. On occasion, he would compete against other priests in a food event called the "Collar-nary Cookoff!"

Now at St. Rita, where there is no professional kitchen, he makes soups in the rectory kitchen for his parishioners. These include bean soup or split pea soup, which he brings to the parish and serves in pint-sized containers so everyone can eat at church or take it home for a later meal.

"They love my soups—lentil, seven-bean, corn-and-tomato with rice (see recipe below). I don't like watery soups, but something more substantial."

Although alligator is a common dish in Louisiana, Father Bill has never prepared it. But that might change. "In the fields around here, in the coulee (a natural drainage), people tend to stay in their car or on their tractors. When you live near alligators, you have to be aware. I have never cooked an alligator, but you can eat them during Lent, so we'll see—maybe one day I'll prepare one. Our local turtles get to be really big too, maybe two feet across. They are plentiful, so when there are too many, we make turtle soup."

Although locals enjoy his cooking treats, what Father is most famous for are his numerous fig dishes: cakes, pies, cookies, even fig ice cream that contains whole canned figs in the mix. And he is renowned for his gumbos, for which he makes various types of roux that showcase the main components, such as chicken, shrimp, or vegetables.

"The roux requires different levels of cooking for different gumbos. For shrimp, I make a blond roux; the heavier the meat, the darker the roux."

While Fr. Bill Melançon deserves his culinary fame, he always thanks his mother for what she taught him. "I cook like my momma did—I don't measure in and I have no clue of the amounts. You have to season the way you want, so you must be flexible, and if I try something new, I make it work myself. I know what I like to taste."

Corn and Tomato Soup with Rice

Always looking for tasty and easier ways of preparing dishes, Father Bill relays this family favorite, which he promises is nutritious and filling.

"The addition of cracked rice is a twist to make a thicker soup. If a thinner soup is desired, then keep rice whole or omit it altogether. You can make cracked rice by putting grains of whole rice in a blender and processing it to make small pieces but no rice powder. Can sizes may vary between 15 and 15.5 ounces. Serve with crackers or crusty bread. This takes about one hour to cook."

MAKES ABOUT ONE GALLON OF SOUP

Ingredients:

- 4 to 6 cups water
- 1 15-ounce can whole kernel sweet corn
- 1 15-ounce can cream-style corn
- 1 15-ounce can diced tomatoes
- 1 10-ounce can diced tomatoes-with-green-chilies
- 2 teaspoons minced garlic
- 2 teaspoons dried minced onion or half a small onion, minced
- 1 teaspoon salt
- ½ teaspoon hot sauce
- 1 cup rice, cracked if desired

Directions:

1. Pour 4 cups water into a large pot. Bring the water to a boil over high heat.
2. Add the sweet corn, cream-style corn, diced tomatoes, and diced tomatoes-with-green-chilies. Bring the mixture back to a boil.
3. Add the garlic, onion, salt, and hot sauce. When the mixture comes to a boil again, add the rice. Stir the mixture regularly, making sure nothing sticks to the bottom of the pot.
4. Reduce the heat to medium and taste for flavor. Add spices if desired. If the soup appears too thick, add more water.
5. Regularly stir and make sure nothing is sticking to the bottom of the pot. Reduce the heat to medium. Taste for flavor and add spices as desired.
6. If soup appears to be getting too thick, add some of the remaining water until it reaches the right consistency.

Cooking
on Camera

Msgr. James Vlaun

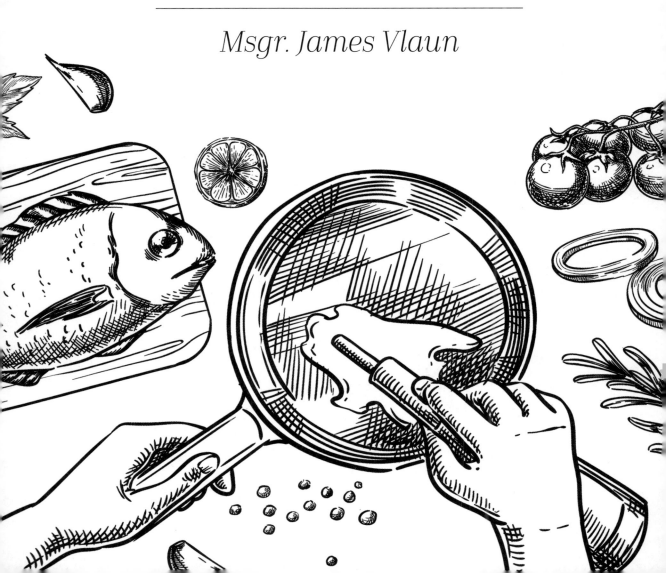

Faith and Music

Born in Queens and raised in Long Island, New York, Msgr. James C. Vlaun grew up in an Italian Catholic family.

Msgr. James Vlaun

"My mother and father were very devout. I grew up in a religious household. We went to church and prayed together, and I went to a Catholic high school."

During his high school years, he began to contemplate a life in the priesthood.

"It was very subtle. That foundational part of life and faith started to become more apparent to me—becoming a priest and helping people. I asked God to help me discern. I went to a Catholic college seminary for undergraduate studies and then to the Seminary of the Immaculate Conception, located in Huntington, New York."

Msgr. Vlaun also credits his devotion to the Blessed Mother and her influence in leading him to the priesthood. He felt an affirmation to use God's gifts as a priest to serve God and the Church. But he knew that in becoming a priest, he would have to give up certain loves, among them, his love of music.

"I grew up in a house with music playing all the time. It was jazz or opera, and there was a love for cooking and gathering people around the table. I figured a lot of that would go away."

He later realized the Lord was probably laughing at him, as the exact opposite happened.

"In my first year in the priesthood, I did a program called 'Religion and Rock.' It consisted of ten rock songs around a particular theme, like unity or forgiveness. I spoke in between the songs, and every six weeks an artist would talk about his or her faith and how God fits into life. It has been on the air for thirty-two years and airs twice a week on Sirius XM on the Catholic Channel. It's been such a blessing to use music, something I love so much, to draw people to God."

Table to Table

Perhaps the young Msgr. Vlaun also did not foresee what other ways God would use him, having him connect not only music with faith but food with faith as well. Just as with music, the groundwork for this was laid during his youth.

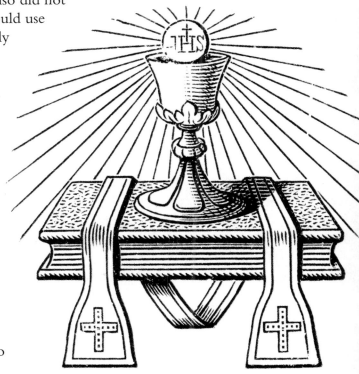

"We lived in a two-family house with my Italian grandparents. On Sundays after Mass, we came home and went upstairs to Grandma's house. Usually, she did the cooking, and I was an observer. I learned a lot from her. Then we had a big Sunday meal. Looking back on it, I truly cherish those meals, even if I didn't at the time."

It won't come as a surprise to know that Msgr. Vlaun's favorite dishes are usually Italian.

"Every Sunday, the menu was the same. We ate rigatoni with tomato gravy made from scratch, baked chicken, and potatoes. It is the simple dishes that Italian peasants make. That is how I grew up, and they are what reminds me of my family life and childhood."

Unlike the fast-paced world of today, Msgr. Vlaun recalls how long they would sit together and how that time together had deeper meaning than just the food they ate.

"We sat at the table for up to five hours sometimes just talking and laughing. The whole day, centered around our meal, became so meaningful.

It was easy to see the connection between those family meals and the Sacred Meal, the Eucharist, we partook of earlier in the day. I am grateful to God for that."

This, he explained, is how he has been able to connect table (the altar) to table (the family meal), adding, "Being around the altar and receiving the Blessed Sacrament made a direct link for me at my earliest age."

"Real Food"

In 1988, Msgr. Vlaun became involved with the Catholic Faith Network (www.CFNtv.org), which has a lengthy history. Formerly known as Telecare TV until 2018, the network was founded in 1969 by Msgr. Thomas Hartman, also of the Diocese of Rockville Centre, New York. Ever since its inception, their focus has been on broadcasting relevant Catholic programs, from live religious services to educational shows. This television network showcases every aspect of Catholicism, from broadcasting a daily Mass to Catholic news to numerous faith-related programs aired throughout the country.

Earning a Masters in Communications while serving at St. Mary's Church in East Islip, New York would prove providential for Msgr. Vlaun. His education led to his early involvement in his radio show and participation at Telecare Television, hosting a program called "On Long Island."

In 2004, he was assigned to Telecare TV as CEO and president, a station that has since been renamed Catholic Faith Network[11] of the Diocese of Rockville Centre, Long Island, New York.

Now Msgr. Vlaun oversees a station that is on traditional cable networks, accessible through the app "CFN," their website, Apple TV, Amazon Fire, and other traditional cable platforms.

"We produce nineteen series on our own. And we have eight bishops and cardinals for whom we produce programs, plus a daily live news show and devotions such as Masses, the Rosary, and Stations of the Cross. The network is on air twenty-four hours a day and airs in all fifty states."

---

[11] See http://www.cfntv.org.

The idea of incorporating a cooking show into the station's programming came up when he took over.

"While discussing our brand, my team thought a program of what to bring to the dinner table would be unique, a cooking show with a Catholic theme. We did three or four trial shows and tested them to see how they would go over."

When viewers loved the cooking shows, Msgr. Vlaun and his staff of thirty-five initiated the series now known as "Real Food." Their website explains how they "bring faith into the kitchen." The show has changed course over the years. His good friend and fellow Catholic cook Lidia Bastianich advised him to keep the format rotating between hosting a guest chef, doing a solo cooking episode, and visiting a new location to explore the culture and food there. This recipe (pun intended!) has served the show well and made it very successful.

Through the years, Msgr. Vlaun has invited onto the show several well-known chefs, including Mary Ann Esposito, "Iron Chef" Billy Gallagher, and the now-deceased Dom Deluise and Frank Pellegrino of Rao's Restaurant, plus others who were less famous but wonderful chefs and cooks in their own right. While the guests do the cooking, Msgr. Vlaun does the talking, trying to bring out religious themes in the food. Most of the guests are Catholic, but some have been from other faiths. When no guest is present, Msgr. Vlaun cooks solo and engages with the audience.

As far as the recipes he uses on "Real Food," some are from his family, while others are of his own creation.

"A common way I develop my own recipes comes from dining out. I can take something and make it my own. That's how we build the recipe collections on the show. When eating out, I write things down and we go from there."

Msgr. Vlaun has also taken some of the cooking shows on the road, to restaurants in Manhattan or on Arthur Avenue in the Bronx, among other locations across the country. He even took the show to Rome, where he visited different restaurants, a ravioli factory, and outdoor farmers' markets.

"The most memorable episodes were the ones I did in Rome. We would go shopping in the morning with all the locals for cheese, tomatoes, and other items. We then took everything to a friend's restaurant and recorded us cooking in his kitchen. Making the link between food and faith while in Rome was not all that difficult!"

Due to his busy schedule, Msgr. Vlaun and his staff consolidate their studio work to an August schedule. "We tape in a block during the summer, and we are so fortunate to work with so many great people. We partner with the Vatican, the USCCB, and a number of archdioceses. We usually tape four shows a day, though the ones on the road we shoot throughout the year."

Real Food has been supported by sponsorship from the Catholic Church and many in the food industry, including national brands like Pomi, Vantia Imports, Ambrosi Parmigiano-Reggiano cheese, Colavita, San Pellegrino, and many others. The show's viewership is diverse and extends beyond just Catholics. The network receives volumes of letters, even from folks who have found the channel while channel surfing. Their show has also inspired other Catholic stations to do their own version.

As he reflects on his faith-and-cooking program, Msgr. Vlaun is thankful for all that God has blessed him with. He also appreciates the support he has received from the Church.

"I am proud that our bishop sees the need for a Catholic television network to serve the Church and devotes a full-time priest to it. We touch millions of lives every day with the Gospel and the Church's teachings, and our ability to share theology and tradition. The cooking show is about Catholic living and family, and how gathering in homes is linked to gathering at Church. We should never forget that or take the time at table together with our family for granted. Those meals are a reflection of the heavenly banquet that awaits us in heaven."

Orecchiette with Asparagus and Peas

This recipe calls for a cheese called Grana Padano, similar in taste to Parmesan, but milder. Its original producers were the Cistercian monks of the Chiaravalle Abbey in Northern Italy.

SERVES 4 TO 6

Ingredients:

- 1 teaspoon kosher salt
- 4 tablespoons extra-virgin olive oil
- 4 cloves garlic, peeled and thinly sliced
- 1 large bunch medium-thick aspara-gus, peeled and cut into 1-inch pieces
- 1 pound orecchiette
- One box frozen peas, thawed
- 1 cup chopped red onions
- ¼ cup chopped fresh Italian parsley
- 1 cup grated Grana Padano cheese

Directions:

1. Bring a large pot of salted water to boil for cooking the pasta.
2. Add 3 tablespoons olive oil to a large skillet over medium heat.
3. When the oil is hot, add the garlic and let it sizzle for one minute.
4. Add the asparagus and cook and toss for about 5 minutes. Remove from the heat and cover.
5. Add the orecchiette to the water.
6. Uncover the asparagus, add the peas and remaining 1 tablespoon salt.
7. Heat over medium heat and toss for 2 to 3 minutes.
8. Add the onions, stir, and add 1½ cups pasta water. Bring to a boil and cook for 3 to 4 minutes.
9. When the pasta is tender, drain and add it directly to the sauce. Add the parsley, drizzle with the remaining olive oil, and mix.
10. Sprinkle with the grated cheese and serve.

Chefs
& Cooks

The Catholic Foodie

Jeff Young

Cooking in the Holy Land

"There I was in the kitchen of Magdalena Restaurant, one of the best restaurants in Palestine, located in Migdal, the hometown of Saint Mary Magdalene, and the owner and chef, Joseph Hanna, is helping me put on an apron as he tells me about the historical dish we would be preparing for the pilgrims' lunch—Saint Peter's Fish. I'm staring at the big white bins filled with fresh-caught tilapia from the Sea of Galilee and the fresh-chopped parsley and green onions and sliced tomatoes in the prep area, and I begin to wonder: How in the world did I get here?"

Jeff Young

Such were the thoughts of Jeff Young, perhaps better known as the Catholic Foodie, in 2014 as he led a food-and-faith pilgrimage to the Holy Land. That pilgrimage became part of the basis of his first book, *Around the Table with the Catholic Foodie: Middle Eastern Cuisine.* As a Holy Land pilgrimage, the attendees engaged in all of the usual elements of a pilgrimage, including visits to all the historic sites tied to the life of Jesus of Nazareth, along with daily Mass at those sites. But as a food-and-faith pilgrimage, the trip also included visits to Christian-owned restaurants, wineries, and a brewery, along with the opportunity to get into the kitchen with chefs and to learn how to make some of the most iconic Middle Eastern dishes.

"I had started *The Catholic Foodie* blog and podcast in 2008. I never thought that anyone would really be all that interested. I was just a geek who loved his faith and loved to cook, so I started writing about food and faith, and talking about it on the podcast."

As it turned out, many were interested in Jeff's musings about faith and food. The blog and podcast grew in popularity, and "Chef Jeff" then branched out into radio, wrote a book, and has contributed to several others (including this one!).

"There's just something about food that speaks to our hearts. I think that's why the Food Network and the Cooking Channel have been so successful, and why we even have such a thing as 'celebrity chefs.'"

Chef Jeff's website[12] averages about a thousand visitors a day, whether he posts anything new or not. He attributes that to the catalog of recipes and faith-building stories published there.

"We are made for communion, and historically we most often find communion around the table, of course around the Eucharist but also around the family table. In a world where technology and busyness have been tearing at the fabric of family life for decades, it takes intentionality to grow and maintain relationships, especially between those under the same roof. Putting away the distractions and getting back into the kitchen together and back around the table is a very effective way for families to connect, to pray together, and to experience communion. I've devoted my life to fostering that reality in as many people as I can."

Making the Magic

Jeff grew up in Baton Rouge, Louisiana in a traditional family setting.

"It was a different era back then, and stay-at-home moms were the normal thing. My mom cooked every day. I had my share of Vienna sausages, deviled ham, and Spam, but most of my meals were home-cooked and delicious. In south Louisiana, an area known the world over for their cuisine—Cajun in the Lafayette area and Creole in New Orleans—it seems like everyone is a cook. I grew up with people just knowing how to cook. For probably the first twelve years of my life, after Mass on Sundays, we would go to my paternal grandparents' house for lunch. All of my cousins and aunts and uncles would be there, and my maw-maw and paw-paw would cook for the whole clan. It was really good formation for both family life and for

---

[12]   See catholicfoodie.com.

cooking. Cooking for me has always been like magic. To take raw ingredients and to make something so yummy with them is just an amazing thing to witness and to taste. But I wasn't satisfied with just witnessing. I wanted to *make* the magic."

Although he would eventually build a repertoire of recipes that includes various gumbos, exotic salads, and classic dishes from a number of countries like Italy, India, Mexico, Lebanon, and Israel, Jeff's beginnings were rather humble.

"I think the first thing I learned to cook was scrambled eggs. But what really captured my heart and what set me on the path to learning how to cook was pizza! I loved pizza—couldn't get enough of it. But, unfortunately, the rest of the family didn't love it as much as I did; at least they didn't have the stamina I did when it came to pizza. Keep in mind, this was way before pizza delivery places like Papa John's and Domino's were around, so it wasn't as common back then. I was able to convince my mom to start buying pizza kits from the grocery store. Chef Boyardee and Appian Way are two of the brands I remember. But it didn't take too long before I started to make my own dough and my own tomato sauce, and use real mozzarella cheese! I am still passionate about pizza today."

Despite his love for cooking, Jeff admits to being a picky eater.

"I was the worst! I couldn't stand beans or most vegetables. If forced to, I would eat an iceberg lettuce salad if it was doused in Wish-Bone Italian Dressing. That and corn. Those were my only two vegetables I would eat for years. Thankfully, my palate has developed since then. I love greens and almost all vegetables. If given an option, I would eat salad for breakfast every morning."

The Sacramental Nature of Meals

Though it took time for him to connect his love of food with his faith, the bond between these two passions drives him each day. This connection between food and faith is part of his unique approach to cooking and why he emphasizes family meals so much.

"Food and faith are two great tastes that taste even better together, like chocolate and peanut butter in Reese's candy. I think my ability to see the connection between food and faith is a God-given gift. It's just part of who I am."

That gift was reinforced through his study of Scripture and theology during two trips into the seminary. At the age of eighteen, Jeff left home and moved to Mexico where he spent two years in formation with Mother Teresa's priests, the Missionaries of Charity Fathers. He returned home after that and went to college for a couple of years, before entering the seminary again to study for the Diocese of Baton Rouge.

"God had different plans for me, though. A couple years after graduating, I married a beautiful and holy Lebanese woman, and we now have four children. My wife, Char, has blessed me in more ways than I can count, but she is also the one who has helped me most when it comes to cooking and eating. I learned so much about cooking from her and her mom. And that was one of the reasons I was so excited to meet Chef Joseph Hanna and to dine in his restaurant, Magdalena. Even though the Holy Land is not Lebanon, the cuisine is virtually the same, so going there was like going back to the culinary roots of my wife's heritage."

There wasn't enough room in the kitchen to accommodate all the pilgrims, so Chef Joseph invited Jeff back to the kitchen to see how the whole tilapia is prepared. What happened next was a happy surprise.

"As we walked back to the kitchen, I mentioned to Chef Joseph that my wife is of Lebanese heritage and that traditional Lebanese dishes frequently appear on our dinner table at home. He nodded his approval because, as it turned out, he was also Lebanese!"

Jeff continues, "When we got to the workstation, there were about twenty whole tilapia, separated four to a tray, that had been gutted, scaled, and scored, waiting to be prepped. Chef Joseph's colleague, Chef Muhammad, demonstrated how they prepared the fish, as Chef Joseph called for a chef's apron to be put on me. The first thing Chef Muhammad did was to liberally salt the inside and the outside of the fish. He followed the salt with coarse-ground black pepper, and then pulled into view a white container with what looked like tabbouleh inside. I said, 'Hey, that's tabbouleh! That looks just like the way we make it at home!' Chef Joseph's face lit up and we started laughing. It was like we were little kids. He was so excited to show me all the different things in his kitchen, the different lettuces and greens, the herbs they use for seasoning, and we tasted everything. I was just eating it all up. Figuratively, I mean. Thankfully, our guide, Arlette, was there to document it all in photographs. I was having a ball."

But the fun would not end there.

"Then Chef Muhammad turned to me and said, 'OK. Now it's your turn.' And he pointed to the remaining fish. I smiled and got to work. I loved it! In the end, I prepared the Saint Peter's Fish for everyone in my group, except for myself, because Chef Joseph wanted to prepare mine."

This experience and many others have led Jeff to a unique vision of sharing a meal with those we love.

"There is something sacramental in the sharing of a meal, and in the preparation of that meal. Magdalena Restaurant wasn't a church or a holy spot, but for me, cooking and dining there was definitely a spiritual experience. Making new friends, sharing a meal around the table, enjoying the goodness of God's providence in the form of good food and good wine, it was all a very real experience of the family of God and of God's presence with us. And that experience is something that can happen around your table and mine. You don't have to be in the Holy Land to experience it. This is what *The Catholic Foodie* is all about. It's where food meets faith. It's why I create Catholic culinary inspiration to help families grow in faith around the table."

Chef Jeff's Tilapia

Jeff relays to us a few basics before laying out the recipe for his tilapia.

"This is one of those 'you gotta eyeball it' recipes. There are lots of variables: the size of the bunches of parsley, the size of the bunch of green onions, etc. It takes practice (and lots of tasting!) to get it just right. So go slow on the olive oil and the lemon juice. Then season with salt and cayenne to taste."

He continues, "On the pilgrimage, each pilgrim was served a whole fish. The ingredient portions I included in the recipe are measured for four to five whole tilapias. If I was serving this to guests in my home, I would prepare a whole fish for each person, or I would serve it family style in the middle of the table, allowing each guest to serve themselves. Keep in mind that whole fish have bones. Eating a whole fish usually necessitates using one's hands!"

Jeff passes along one more special note. "The marinade can be made in advance and stored in the refrigerator for a couple of days before use. Serve the fish alongside roasted vegetables and a salad for the best possible meal. And enjoy!"

Ingredients:

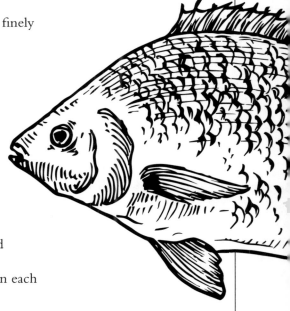

- 1 to 2 bunches of fresh Italian flat-leaf parsley, finely chopped
- 2 to 4 tablespoons fresh finely chopped mint
- 1 bunch green onions, finely chopped
- 1 sweet yellow onion, peeled and finely chopped
- 6 to 8 medium-sized vine tomatoes, diced
- 1/2 cup extra-virgin olive oil
- Juice of 1 to 2 lemons
- 1 teaspoon kosher salt, or to taste, plus additional to season each fish
- 1/2 to 1 teaspoon cayenne pepper, or to taste
- 4 or 5 whole Tilapia, gutted, scaled, and scored 3 times on each side
- Freshly cracked black pepper, to taste, to season each fish
- 4 or 5 large sprigs of rosemary

Directions:

1. Add the chopped and diced vegetables to a large glass bowl.
2. Add the olive oil and lemon juice and mix well. Cover with plastic wrap and refrigerate for at least 1 hour so the flavors can marry.
3. Preheat the oven to 400 degrees.
4. Take a tilapia and season it generously inside and out (and both sides) with salt and black pepper, making sure that you season inside the scoring marks too.
5. Using a large serving spoon, scoop a generous amount of the marinade into the cavity of the fish, then add more marinade to the top of the fish, working it into the score marks with your hands.
6. Finally, add some of the rosemary to the fish, inside and out. Repeat this process with the remaining fish.
7. Place fish on a large baking tray and bake in the oven at 400 for 30 minutes or until fish flakes. Serve hot.

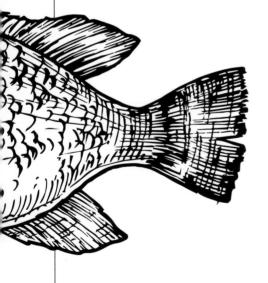

The Filipino Chef

Evelyn Bunoan

The Front of the Class

Evelyn Bunoan is a small woman, but what she lacks in size she makes up for in intensity. And it is this intensity that has made her one of the best chefs around.

Evelyn's first baking attempt was an exercise in futility when she pulled a cake from the oven that was more akin to a cinderblock. But this experience of failure drove her to want to get better. She was more determined than ever to pursue the finer side of the culinary arts and enrolled at the Le Cordon Bleu culinary school in London.

Evelyn Bunoan

While there, she always arrived early for class so she could sit in the front row, and she was quick to raise her hand whenever the teacher asked for a volunteer. But for some reason, during breaks from class, she would return to find her stuff moved to the back; apparently, some classmates thought it would be funny to play a prank on her, or they were simply threatened by her drive. Being shy as she was, she never asked anyone about it but would simply move back up to the front of the class where she had been.

Her determination during the course of her culinary endeavor led her to be among the top three students during cooking exams. She eventually became popular among her classmates and made many friends. Then, lo and behold, whenever she arrived in class, the best seat was reserved for her up front, and she became the primary source of advice for others. The lessons she learned in London would serve her well for the remainder of her life.

Life in Rosario

Though Evelyn currently resides in Northern Virginia where she runs a mini grocery store, carryout, and catering business, her story began on the other side of the world.

"I was born in the Philippines in the town of Rosario, Cavite in Luzon, about sixteen miles south of Manila."

The strength of her family's Catholic faith was a strong influence on her. Her mother used to walk the sixteen miles from her town to Manila as a devotion to God and to pray in the local church. The surrounding culture also influenced Evelyn's faith. Rosario, which has grown in recent years, is close to 100 percent Roman Catholic.

"Our patron saint is Our Lady of the Rosary (*Santo Rosario*). According to local legend, there was a miracle in the past because some fishermen and

residents saw the statue of the Virgin Mary in the sea. My mother told me they could see the image of the Virgin from the town."

Even today, when Evelyn and her husband visit the town, the church is packed each weekend.

"Whenever we go to visit, we cannot even get a seat because the church is so full. The people there are so devoted."

Philippine Oriental Market & Deli

As a young adult, Evelyn left the Philippines to join her then husband, an accountant, as an immigrant. Upon arrival in the United States, she applied for work at the World Bank and got a job that eventually qualified her as an executive assistant to the auditor general.

"I had majored in accounting and minored in marketing at the University of the East in Manila where I studied for six years. I was a working student as a stenographer and eventually as audit examiner at the Department of Labor, helping to send my brothers and sisters to college."

In 1978, now in the United States, she bought a Filipino store and let her close relatives help her operate it during the weekdays while she worked at the World Bank so that she could manage it on weekends.

"I bought the store during Holy Week. Most Filipinos don't work then, in observance of the last week of Lent, so we opened after Easter Sunday."

After almost twenty-eight years at the World Bank, Evelyn decided to focus on the store—now called Philippine Oriental Market & Deli, or POM—in Arlington, Virginia. Initially just a grocery store well stocked with Filipino goods and ingredients, the market gradually evolved into a mini-restaurant that also offers carry out. This second phase of the business was brought about in large part because of Evelyn's foresight. She envisioned "food-to-go" becoming the next trend, so she invested in a commercial kitchen and started offering Filipino dishes, many of which were her own creations and became instant hits. The store was subsequently featured in the Best Bites column of the *Washingtonian* magazine after its success.

Evelyn credits her culinary talents to cooking with her mother, though their experience in the kitchen was not like most. Growing up, her family did not have an oven but rather had to build a fire to heat up their food. Her father, meanwhile, as a professional baker, also had his own talents. She remembers him coming home with a very special Filipino bread called *pan de sal*. Although she does not have her father's recipe, she has created the bread from memory.

"It's made with wheat flour, salt, and yeast. You can just play around with the dough by adding other healthy ingredients."

Evelyn bakes and sells this bread by request at her store, and it is very popular. Most of the dishes she prepares fresh each day for the hot bar. She also stocks freshly cooked food, desserts, and pastries in the refrigerated food-to-go section. While most of her prepared foods are Filipino in origin, some possess a French touch, and she has incorporated other offerings to appeal to customers of different ethnicities.

"Since I opened the market in 1978, I started cooking healthy foods, and thought of myself as a pioneer, of which I was recognized by Filipina Women's Network in 2009 as one of the 100 Most Influential Filipina Women in the United States. Other places were not serving healthy foods back then. At first, my customers were laughing and saying, 'No fat in the meat or chicken?' Now they are praising me. I have had customers for thirty to forty years with no health issues, and they credit my food in part for that."

The Ambassador's Chef

Over the years, one of her most notable customers was the former Philippine Ambassador to the United States, Jose L. Cuisia Jr. In 2011, she was recommended to the ambassador and his wife, Vicky.

"They needed a chef, and I was called by the ambassador's wife. They liked what I delivered, so I would cook for them frequently upon request. Then I became their permanent chef for about four years."

For special events, Evelyn would email a menu proposal to Vicky and go from there.

"Very seldom would they change the menu. Most of their guests would be other ambassadors or senators, or White House staff or dignitaries from the Philippines. I would usually cook the meals ahead in my store kitchen, though sometimes I would cook in the ambassador's residence, but I would always style the five courses."

As expected, Evelyn prepared mostly authentic Filipino dishes, many her own recipes with her unique style.

"We would deliver the food upstairs to the residence kitchen," she recalls, adding that one of the most popular entrées was the tenderloin. "I have a lot of recipes for that. One is braised or stuffed filet mignon with a red wine and mushroom sauce, or sometimes I would prepare my own recipe of a baked jumbo crab meat entrée with lemon juice and herbs. Their favorite dessert was tiramisu made from scratch."

Some of the ambassador's favorite dishes are also favorites at the store.

"When I cook shrimp with squash and coconut milk for the market, it sells out in a few minutes. Another favorite is the Filipino chicken *sisig*. The traditional *sisig* version is made with the head of the pig, but my own version is made with boneless chicken thighs seasoned with lemon pepper and herb seasonings. And, of course, the *lechon* (roast pork). Ours is different from the traditional *lechon* that is cooked over live coals. Instead, I boil the pork until tender and roast in a turbo roaster."

Cooking for Others

Inspired by her Catholicism to always help others, twenty years ago Evelyn started the CHEW Foundation (Cancer Help Eat Well). To help a best friend who was dying of lung cancer, she began this foundation, for which she cooks and delivers meals to cancer patients in need.

"I have known some of these customers for forty years. They are just like family. In their first stage of illness, I always cook healthy food, and when they are in remission, I tell them not to eat fatty or sweet foods. When they get to stage IV, I tell them just to eat what they want. I don't want to deprive them. I had a priest with melanoma and now he is in remission. He gave up red meat and sweets, and I gave him vegetarian/vegan foods."

After so many years in the kitchen, which dish or recipe is her favorite?

"I love all of them," she says, though as a simple person, she usually keeps her home kitchen stocked with avocados, sweet potatoes, and mushrooms—and no junk food in her refrigerator, only celery, parsley, bok choi, Shanghai cabbage, spinach, and kale.

Though she enjoys local fame for her cooking, the most important thing to Evelyn Bunoan is the Catholic faith. She and her husband pray the Rosary every day. "We never miss. We pray before we eat, after eating, and before we sleep. The prayers have made our marriage strong. We love each other; we forgive every day. This is what we are called to do as children of God."

Squash Braised in Coconut Milk with Jumbo Shrimp

Evelyn wished to share one of her unique dishes with us.

"This is one of my dishes that became an instant hit. The following step-by-step procedures will make preparation for this squash recipe a lot easier."

She goes on to explain that kabocha squash is a winter squash that tastes similar to a sweet potato and is a delicious addition to soups and stews. Saffron water, which can be bought at most Asian stores and markets, enhances the color and character of the dish. Its use is optional. A pinch of yellow food coloring is a ready substitute.

SERVES 6 TO 8

Ingredients:

- 1 1/2 pounds kabocha squash
- 2 cups coconut milk
- 1/2 cup water
- 2 teaspoons saffron water, optional
- 30 jumbo shrimp, fresh or frozen, peeled and deveined
- 3 sweet peppers, julienned
- Salt and white pepper to taste

Directions:

1. To prepare the squash, clean it under running water, removing any imperfections on the surface. Wipe it dry.
2. On a cutting board, use a chef's knife and cut the squash in half lengthwise through the stalk. Lay the cut side of the squash down on the cutting board, slice the half lengthwise along the grooves and cut into bite-sized portions.
3. Scrape out the seeds and the pulp. Repeat on the other half. Cut each portion into bite-sized pieces.
4. To cook the squash, add the coconut milk to a large saucepan and bring it to a boil over medium heat.
5. Reduce the heat to low and cook for about 10 minutes, or until the milk has thickened.
6. Add the squash, water, and saffron water or yellow food coloring, and season with salt and pepper.
7. Cook the squash until half-cooked.
8. Add the shrimp and cook until pinkish, about 5 minutes. Do not overcook.
9. Add the sweet peppers and continue cooking for 2 to 3 minutes more. Serve hot.

The Cajun
Chef

John Folse

A Cajun Childhood

Louisiana native son Chef John Folse was blessed to be born on River Road in St. James Parish, a Catholic- and food-centric community in the heart of Cajun country. Chef Folse has garnered a national reputation for his faith and his culinary skills and attributes his life achievements to his devout family upbringing.

John Folse

Of French- and German-Catholic descent, John tells of former times when many of his German forebearers arrived in the Louisiana Colony on Les Deux Freres' ship in March 1721. His ancestor, Johan Michael Zerhinger, was commissioned to build the first Ursuline Convent, as well as the Church of St. Louis, where St. Louis Cathedral stands today in the New Orleans French Quarter.

"The Catholic Church was the center of our lives. The pastor at St. James Catholic Church used to visit our home often. The priest visited all of the families in our neighborhood—that was common back then. I remember him visiting when I had my gall bladder removed and I remember his larger-than-life-presence when my mother died. I think about how often he visited our home. Most times, he would sit and eat a bowl of gumbo with us."

John grew up in a tight-knit community surrounded by a strong, extended family of grandparents, great-grandparents, aunts, uncles, and cousins—all of which had a tremendous impact on his life and faith. The Church was at the center of faith, family, and community activities.

"As soon as we were old enough, we all became altar boys. I started at the age of seven or eight and served until the end of high school. Mass was in Latin back then, and we sometimes went more than once a day."

Like most Louisianans, John spent much of his upbringing in the out-doors. The family lived near a swamp where his father and others trapped alligators, turtles, mink, and fox; what they did not trap, they hunted. Thus, it was not unusual for the family's ice box to be filled with fur and feathers. Periodically, his dad would be away for months on end capturing pelts for money and meat to feed his large family.

"We were taught to be respectful of the land and the animals that pro-vided sustenance for our family."

John's father, in addition to teaching his family about their Catholic faith and how to live off the land, wanted his children to understand the traditions and techniques of Cajun cooking. In fact, John is not the only cook in his family; to this day, his brothers gather to hold huge crawfish boils that bene-fit local churches, schools, and families.

A Saint Knocks on the Door

Looking back on his life, John credits two people who inspired his culinary passion and training.

"My mom was a fabulous cook, but she died in 1955. So someone else would end up helping my dad raise me and my siblings. Mary Ferchaud, an African-American woman living in the area, who had a large family her-self, met my very pregnant mother on a hot, humid morning when mother was hanging clothes on the line. Mary sat my mother down on the steps and hung the clothes. Mom reached up, grabbed her hand, and said, 'Thank you. If anything happens to me, I pray someone like you will look in on my children.' A short time later, my mother died in childbirth, and Mary came knocking on the door. She told my dad that she was there to care for the children, explaining that she had promised his deceased wife she would help if anything ever happened to her. Divine Providence sent us a saint."

Although John's brothers were all good marksmen and spent their time firing guns with their dad, his skillset would be honed at Mary's apron strings.

"For twenty years she cooked breakfasts of rice and eggs. She made dinner. She washed our clothes. And, most importantly, she loved us like a mother. Seeing as how she was named after the Virgin Mother, that seemed fitting."

John continues, "While my brothers hunted, I watched Mary cook. I was maybe ten years old when she taught me about scallions. She had me look at it with its little roots and told me to cut them off. Mary said, 'And when you cut off the roots, you're cooking.'"

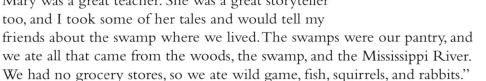

John can't help but smile when he considers now that his entire culinary company is based on how to cut roots off scallions.

"I was a pretty good cook by the time I was twelve. I'm not saying I was a good student, but Mary was a great teacher. She was a great storyteller too, and I took some of her tales and would tell my friends about the swamp where we lived. The swamps were our pantry, and we ate all that came from the woods, the swamp, and the Mississippi River. We had no grocery stores, so we ate wild game, fish, squirrels, and rabbits."

John sings the praises not only of Mary's kitchen training but also the additional religious education he received sitting around the kitchen table and listening to her stories.

"Mary was a big storyteller and most of her stories were about faith and her community. Her family attended St. James Catholic Church, just as we did."

Mary stayed with the family until the youngest children graduated from high school, saying proudly that her promise was fulfilled and her job was done.

"When she died many years later, her funeral Mass was at that little church, and my five brothers and I were her pallbearers. She's buried not far from mother. The community that gathered that day all knew her commitment to the Folse family. What she had accomplished was amazing. She was a gift from God and a saint to all of us."

Becoming Chef John Folse

Chef John Folse's first professional step towards his cooking career started when he was hired by the now-shuttered Prince Murat Hotel in Baton Rouge when he was twenty-six years old. Though he worked in the front of the house,[13] he often hung out in the kitchen of the hotel restaurant where he met a German chef.

"I brought my lunch to work one day, and he asked to taste it. He loved the nuance of flavors and told me I needed to cook. I never dreamed of being a professional chef, but under his guidance, I am who I am today."

By 1978, John had gained enough culinary training and encouragement to launch Chef John Folse & Company. His first restaurant was Lafitte's Landing Restaurant, located at the foot of the Sunshine Bridge.

Today, he is managing partner at Restaurant R'evolution, located in New Orleans's French Quarter, as well as at Folse Market in the New Orleans Airport. He has also opened numerous international restaurants. In 1988, John made international headlines with the

---

[13] "Front of the house" in a restaurant refers to the host stand, waiting area, bar, outdoor seating, etc. while "back of the house" refers to the chefs and prep crew.

opening of "Lafitte's Landing East" in Moscow during the Presidential Summit between Ronald Reagan and Mikhail Gorbachev. And in 1989, he was the first non-Italian chef to create a Vatican State Dinner in Rome. Other promotional restaurants include London in 1991 and 1993, Bogota in 1991, Taipei in 1992 and 1994, and Seoul in 1994.

"Sometimes I wonder: How in the world did I get here? My God, this is impossible."

Through the years, he has learned that his Catholic faith can impact every single person. While preparing for the Russia restaurant opening, his translator confided that she was Catholic and desired to have a Bible. Against all odds, John smuggled a Bible into Russia for her.

"I realized that I had not gone to Russia to open a restaurant; I went to Russia to deliver God's Word to a fellow Catholic."

In addition to his international efforts, John also owns a food processing plant, creating soups, sauces, entrées, and bakery items for international distribution, as well as a catering facility called White Oak Estate & Gardens. He has published ten cookbooks and hosts *A Taste of Louisiana* on PBS. Of all his accomplishments though, which also include numerous national and international culinary and business accolades, it is the Chef John Folse Culinary Institute at Nicholls State University that he considers to be his legacy.[14]

And what, after all his travels, recipe creations, and cooking experiences, is his favorite recipe?

14 CJFCI was founded by former NSU President Donald Ayo and Chef John Folse with the Louisiana Board of Regents approval. CJFCI began offering courses for college credit in 1995. The institute accepted its inaugural academic class in January 1996, offering an associate of science degree. The Board of Regents authorized Nicholls to offer a bachelor's degree in culinary arts in 1997, making it the first four-year culinary degree program at a US public university. Chef Folse has always told his students, "You will make the Culinary Institute known by your work ethic and success in the workplace." Today, graduates of CJFCI own restaurants, are research and development chefs at prominent food companies, and are involved in food media. Annually, six to nine outstanding students spend their summer at Institut Paul Bocuse in Lyon, France with other students from around the globe. CJFCI is the only culinary program in the United States to be a member of the Institut Paul Bocuse Worldwide Alliance.

"I like regional Cajun dishes, especially my Wild Duck, Andouille, and Oyster Gumbo. Gumbo is the major 'soup' in Cajun country. Everybody has their own version and every one of them is delicious!"

Chef John Folse has certainly put Louisiana and its Cajun foods onto the national stage, but his Catholic achievements in his home state have made an impact as well. He is a supporter of Saint Vincent de Paul, a frequent speaker at Catholic organizations, and is a supporter of the Mercedarian Sisters of the Blessed Sacrament at Cypress Springs Mercedarian Prayer Center in Baton Rouge. Sister Dulce Maria, who was inspired by God to build the center, works with the sick, dying, and terminally ill. Chef Folse is president of the Sister Dulce Foundation, Inc.

To have the strength and will to maintain his busy schedule, he relies on daily prayer.

"I begin my day with prayer and morning Scripture readings. Then throughout the day, I remember to thank God for my faith, my family, all the gifts of this life, and of course, all the places He has yet to lead me. I can't wait for what's next."

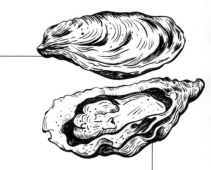

Wild Duck, Andouille, and Oyster Gumbo

John has been kind enough to pass along his favorite recipe to us.

"Almost every species of wild game in Louisiana have been used in the creation of gumbo. Since most Cajun men are hunters, it's not surprising that the day's kill is quite often used in the evening meal. Many hunters prefer mallard duck and smoked andouille gumbo. It's a fantastic dish."

SERVES 12
Preparation time is about 1½ hours

Ingredients:

- 1 cup vegetable oil
- 1½ cups flour
- 2 cups diced onions
- 1 cup diced celery
- 1 cup diced bell peppers
- ¼ cup minced garlic
- 2 mallard ducks, cut into serving pieces
- 2 pounds andouille sausage, sliced

- 3 quarts chicken stock
- 12 chicken livers
- 2 pints select oysters, optional
- 2 cups sliced green onions
- 1 cup chopped parsley
- Salt and freshly ground black pepper to taste
- Louisiana hot sauce to taste
- Steamed white rice

Directions:

1. In a 2-gallon stockpot, heat the oil over medium-high heat.
2. Whisk in the flour, stirring constantly, until a golden-brown roux is achieved.
3. Stir in onions, celery, bell peppers, and garlic.
4. Sauté 3 to 5 minutes or until the vegetables are wilted.
5. Fold in the duck and andouille.
6. Sauté about 15 minutes.
7. Add the chicken stock, one ladle at a time, stirring constantly.
8. Bring to a rolling boil, reduce the heat to medium-low, and stir in the chicken livers and oysters.
9. Cook 1 hour, adding stock as needed until the duck is tender.
10. Sprinkle in green onions and parsley. Season to taste with salt, pepper, and hot sauce.
11. Cook an additional 5 minutes and serve over steamed white rice.

A Lover
of Catholic
Culture

Jennifer Gregory Miller

Life in a Catholic Home

If you do a web search for a Jennifer Miller, you will come up with a bearded circus performer, a jewelry maker, an actress, a dentist, and a college professor, among a few others named Jennifer Miller. But the name you might not see is this: Jennifer Gregory Miller—a wife, mother of two sons, Catholic author, catechist at a Catholic Montessori school, a talented home cook, and a staff member of the Northern Virginia-based website CatholicCulture.org.[15]

Now a resident of Manassas, Virginia, Jennifer is a native Texan, born and raised in Houston. Her family later moved to Shreveport, Louisiana, and then to Manassas. All three of these very different regions formed who she has become as an adult.

"We were surrounded by family in Texas, so we built a close-knit relationship, marking family celebrations together. Northern Louisiana did not have the same Catholic roots and culture. I had to learn more about being Catholic, enabling me to defend my faith. My family then moved to Virginia when I was nineteen."

The fact that both her parents took their Catholic faith seriously also helped lay her spiritual foundation.

"My father was in a Carmelite seminary, but when he decided that was not his vocation, he left and eventually met my mom. He was always leading a liturgical life and still prays the Divine Office in Latin."

Her mother's family was from New Orleans where many Catholics lived their faith, often without questioning anything. But when they moved to Houston, where there were less Catholics, Jennifer's mother began to wonder about many of her family's religious traditions, like abstaining from meat on Friday and eating fish dinners instead.

"My mother was seeking those answers, so she formed us with that inquisitive mindset. We had the traditions, but we also needed to know *why* we were doing them. We went to weekly Mass, and sometimes to daily Mass. We prayed the Rosary and we lived our faith very deeply. During Holy

---

[15] See https://www.catholicculture.org.

Week, we attended the Triduum services, but at home we did a bit more to echo the liturgy. For example, on Holy Thursday, we had a meal, an imitation of the Last Supper with lamb. We read the Mass readings and washed each other's feet."

Catholic Culture

Another Catholic tradition her mother taught them was through cooking special recipes. "My mother married at the age of eighteen, and, surprisingly, she couldn't even boil water. But her mother-in-law taught her how to cook. My grandmother had a Scotch/German heritage and loved to read cookbooks and collect recipes. She was very frugal, making wonderful meals on a shoestring budget. She created the food memories that our family has, like her pot roast and cream puffs."

Jennifer's mother had collected several recipes tied to Catholic holidays, and the Saint Nicholas Dutch spice cookies she made became a family tradition on Saint Nicholas day.

"That was part of learning about the faith through cooking. Teachers were surprised when we went to school knowing these traditions when other children did not."

Since Jennifer was the oldest in a family of seven children, she pitched in to help her mother cook. "I started taking over the cooking to help out, and reading her Catholic cookbooks. I didn't know it at the time, but this laid the foundation for what I would do as an adult—working to spread Catholic culture through Catholicculture.org."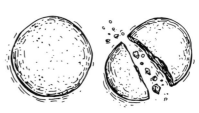

Jennifer started working for *Catholic Culture*'s founder, Jeffrey Mirus, when she was fresh out of high school. Mirus had started the business as a Catholic book publishing company. But he initiated the website when he got involved in internet startups.

"He started a Catholic online site, and it expanded to this idea of *Catholic Culture*, a name inspired by now-deceased Christopher Dawson's

Christian Culture initiative. Why not have the name as *Catholic Culture*? We can share how we can live our Catholic culture and our faith in our day-to-day life by providing examples on how we live, eat, drink, and pray, both historically and currently. This was our venture to make a Catholic imprint in the internet world."

For those who follow the Northern Virginia-based website and love cooking, they have likely scrolled down to the heading "Liturgical Year." Listed there is the title "Recipes," a folder containing scores of Catholic recipes for the liturgical year. Here, website users can easily find ways to celebrate the many feast days of the Church. Jennifer realized that cooking the special liturgical recipes would connect one with the past and present Universal Church.

"I started uploading topics of various interests, such as the liturgical year and cookbooks. We wanted to give the historical aspect and the richness of traditions since Old Testament times. When we started, so many sources were out of print. I was scanning and editing texts to post them online. It was an incredible amount of work, but also very edifying and enriching."

Jennifer tries to refine the recipe section and keep it fresh and new, though she admits she has not been able to test all the new recipes yet.

"I do go back and post tried-and-true recipes. So for Saint Nicholas' feast day on December 6, we have the Speculaas (or *Speculatius*) cookies from Florence Berger's cookbook, *Cooking for Christ*, which has always been my favorite liturgical cookbook."

But she has also found ways to tweak recipes for modern-day cooks: on her personal blog, *Family in Feast and Feria,*[16] she noted a cookbook that had a pot roast for Saint Joseph's Day but adapted it so it would cook in a slow cooker.

"I twist ideas to make recipes adaptable. Even if there isn't a specific recipe or food for a feast or saint's day, I think of ways to incorporate foods that can be a reminder of the saint, such as making something Italian for an Italian saint."

---

[16] See https://familyfeastandferia.com/.

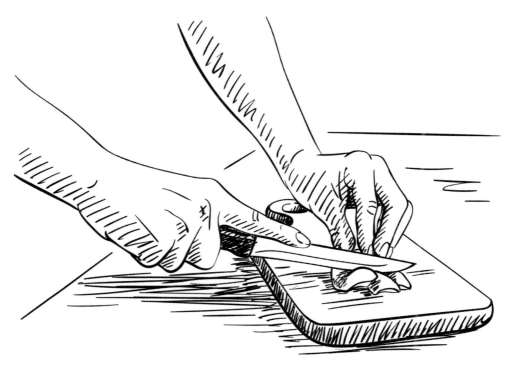

Cooking at Home

So how does Jennifer approach cooking for her family at home?

"When my sons were younger, I found that if they were involved in the process of helping in our vegetable garden, they would eat the vegetables. If I made soup, and they were involved with cutting vegetables, then they were more willing to eat the soup. There was something about helping prepare the food that made them more interested in it. It was a great lesson."

Part of her cooking journey within the home has revolved around food allergies her older son has to wheat, dairy, and tree nuts (and for many years, he also had to avoid eggs).

"His allergies have somewhat hampered my cooking outreach. When my husband and I got married, I would try a new bread recipe for each Christmas and Easter. And then I could not even have flour in the air because my son would get hives and asthma. That cut down on my creativity and it was very discouraging. He loves what I make for him, but I know what the original recipe is supposed to be, so I am not satisfied. Even with Creole dishes, I cannot use a roux, so I use other thickeners, such as okra and *filé* powder (made from ground and dried sassafras leaves). I really wanted to do more creative cooking, and instead my focus had to shift to creating 'safe' foods in a 'safe' kitchen. For big family holidays such as Thanksgiving, I would have to keep him out of the kitchen while I baked pies."

Whatever she ends up cooking, Jennifer is happy to have her husband by her side.

"He knows his way around the kitchen. He says to me, 'Just show me how to do it and I will do it.' He is very matter-of-fact and thinks if you can read, you can cook. In our discussions, I say, 'Yes, you can follow a recipe, but is it really knowing how to cook?' Salting to taste, knowing what spices to use, tweaking a recipe when you don't have everything written down, recognizing by smell when something is done . . . *that* is true cooking."

Her own personal favorites are southern Louisiana-style recipes, though she finds them more time-consuming to make and more elaborate.

"Usually during the week, my meals are very functional and allergy safe, and I try to get them done in an hour. I'm a teacher, so I'm often very tired when I come home. Sometimes you just don't have the energy to make something special or fun, and that's okay."

Her other favorite cuisines are French and northern Italian dishes. But in the end, she is making her own culinary heritage. "I'm creating my own recipes based on traditions from my great-great aunts' or great-grandmothers' cooking heritage, just taking what they did and adding to them or tweaking them."

For her family, faith and food meet at a crossroads that binds them together.

"We eat together as much as we can. That was one thing my mom stressed constantly. We are eating together as a family, and that is keeping our relationship as a family alive. The sharing of the meal is the center of our family life, and the bridge to so many celebrations within the liturgical year.

I tie it all around our family dinner meal. Thankfully, my sons are active in their faith. They attend Catholic schools, and because we have always lived the liturgical year in our home, they always know what feast day it is. With boys, food is the way they think. My sons and husband are always thinking about the next meal, so cooking is the way I tie in living the liturgical year."

Chicken Creole

Jennifer is excited to share with us one of her favorite dishes.

"My comfort meals of choice are south Louisiana cuisine, either Cajun or Creole. All sorts of debates arise on defining Cajun or Creole, but in the food category, Creole usually means it can include tomatoes. This is a skillet meal or can be made in a Dutch oven. Chicken Creole fits the criteria of a comfort meal: quick and easy, and low on the budget. I often make it with chicken thighs, bone-in or boneless, but also a whole chicken cut-up, or already cut-up chicken parts. I usually cook eight chicken thighs, bone-in or boneless, for a family of four, and sprinkle salt over all the chicken pieces before cooking. For the canned tomatoes, if unsalted, be sure to add salt when cooking. Also, if desired, use frozen okra, about twelve to twenty-four ounces. Serve over cooked rice; I usually use Jasmine white rice. Biscuits or cornbread or a sliced French baguette are a nice addition with the meal. To adjust for dairy and wheat allergies, omit butter and flour.""

SERVES 4

Ingredients:

- 2 tablespoons olive oil or unsalted butter
- 3 to 3 1/2 pounds chicken, either whole or chicken parts, or 4 bone-in breasts, or 8 bone-in or boneless thighs
- 1 medium-sized yellow onion, peeled and diced (about 1 to 1 1/2 cups)
- 4 to 5 stalks celery, chopped (about 1 cup)
- 2 to 3 garlic cloves, peeled and coarsely chopped
- Optional: 2 tablespoons all-purpose flour

- ½ to 1 cup dry white wine
- ½ to 1 cup chicken broth
- 1 16-ounce can chopped tomatoes, undrained and salted
- 1 teaspoon salt plus more to taste
- 1 teaspoon dried thyme leaves
- 2 bay leaves
- 1 green bell pepper, seeded and chopped
- 1 or 2 12-ounce bags frozen cut okra
- 4 to 8 dashes Tabasco sauce or other hot pepper sauce

Directions:

Traditional Version

1. Prepare a whole chicken by cutting it into parts, such as legs and thighs; cut the breast in half with wings attached to one side. Try to cut all pieces evenly. If using already cut-up chicken parts, cut chicken breast in half.
2. In a 12-inch or larger lidded skillet, heat the oil or butter over medium heat. Sauté the chicken pieces until golden brown on all sides. Remove the chicken from the skillet and set aside.
3. Add the onion and celery to the skillet and soften; after about 2 minutes, add the garlic. Sauté until soft. Optional: blend in flour until smooth.
   Note: If you prefer to have a "saucier" dish, add the larger amounts of wine and broth, or use smaller amounts if you want less liquid.
4. Add wine to skillet and stir for about 1 or 2 minutes to heat.
5. Add the chicken broth, tomatoes, thyme, bay leaves, and salt. Stir ingredients well and add the chicken.
6. Bring to a boil, then reduce the heat to low and simmer for about 20 minutes.
7. Add the green pepper, okra and Tabasco sauce, and cook for 25 minutes more, or until the chicken is tender. Serve over white rice.

Dutch Oven Version

Preheat oven to 350 degrees F.

1. Sauté chicken and onion, celery and garlic, and cook wine as directed above, then add all the ingredients except okra and Tabasco into the large Dutch oven.
2. Bake for 30 minutes, then add the okra and Tabasco, stir and bake for another 20–30 minutes, or until chicken is tender.

Option 1: Add another layer of flavor by including about 1/2 cup cubed pancetta or salt pork or bacon after the onions, celery, and garlic are softened. Brown and remove excess fat, if necessary, then continue with the remainder of the steps.

Option 2: Add a cup of cubed ham or Kielbasa (Polish Sausage) or Cajun Andouille (spicier addition) and follow the directions for Option 1.

Cornbread

Jennifer offers us a second recipe for cornbread that complements the chicken.

"This cornbread makes for a nice addition to the chicken. The amount of sugar varies by personal taste. I prefer it not too sweet, but just a touch. Omit completely if you prefer savory cornbread. I have successfully made this wheat and dairy free by switching out the flour and butter and milk with allergy-free ingredients."

SERVES 6

Ingredients:

- 1 cup all-purpose flour
- 3/4 cup white or yellow corn meal
- 1 tablespoon to 1/4 cup sugar★
- 1 tablespoon baking powder
- 3/4 teaspoon salt

- 1/2 cup melted butter
- 1 cup whole milk
- 1 large egg, beaten
- 1 stick butter, not melted

Directions:

1. Preheat oven to 425 degrees F. Grease a 9 x 9 x 2-inch pan or a tin for 12 muffins.
2. Whisk all ingredients except the un-melted butter until all lumps are removed. Do not over mix. Pour into greased pan or muffin tins.
3. Bake at 425 degrees F for about 20 to 25 minutes, or until the middle springs back to touch.
4. After removing from oven, while still very hot, slice pats of butter and spread around the top of the cornbread to melt the butter over the whole pan or each muffin. I use about ½ stick, rubbing it over the whole topside. Slice when cooler and serve with butter.

★ Adjust to personal taste.

The Café Evangelist

Ever Johnson

A Devout Family

Ever Johnson's story begins with her name.

"I'm named after both my mother and my grandmother. Ever is a figure in Celtic mythology, the wife of the demigod warrior, Cuchulainn. My parents Christianized it with a Hebrew middle name, Elizabeth, so altogether it means 'forever the house of God.'"

From these unique origins, Ever would later be inspired to begin a career in the food industry thanks to Pope Saint John Paul II. It was the late pontiff's call to evangelize the culture that inspired her and her husband, Soren, to open the non-profit Trinity House Café + Market in Leesburg,

Ever Johnson

Virginia in 2014. What the couple launched, which appears much like a Catholic family home, provides a welcoming setting for all people—regardless of their faith—to gather, eat, and relax.

Although now a Virginia resident, Ever is a native Texan, born in Fort Worth to a devout Catholic family.

"When my parents met at Loyola University of New Orleans, it was the late 1960s and the culture was going crazy. But as 'straight arrow' oldest children, they were having none of that."

When the couple married and moved back to Texas, they remained strong Catholics, gradually growing a family of twelve children (yes, *twelve*!).

"My mom is a creative person, a poet with great depth of feeling. So her expression of the faith was very rich."

While her mom oriented their home toward beauty, she also sang and explained the faith in delightful ways that showed how God's presence both undergirds and crowns daily life. There were saint statues around the house, and Ever fondly remembers her mother dressing the Infant Jesus of Prague for the liturgical season.

"But Mom didn't only show her faith at home. She went to daily Mass at our downtown parish and would often bring home a person in need. Whether she encountered them just briefly for a meal and a heart-to-heart, or they became part of our day-to-day community, Mom never met a needy person she didn't befriend. It's hard to imagine having twelve kids and still having that much heart, but Mom's love doesn't know many limits."

Meanwhile, Ever's dad constantly had his nose in books, engaging the kids in a more intellectual way. He made television off limits for years at a time, reading to the kids and encouraging them to take up books and music. He convened the family for a nightly Rosary, teaching them to pray—for individuals, for the family, for the community, for the country, and for the world—calling on one child after another to lead the prayer.

"And when Sunday came around, he'd be in the van honking while Mom was still trying to see if we were decently dressed for Mass," Ever laughs.

Her parents also dedicated each child to the Blessed Mother, which she believes, besides her parents' example, is the reason why they all remain faithful Catholics today.

"We experienced our parents living out the faith and it took deep root. What they presented—though far from perfect—was so noticeably beautiful, true, and good. When you're formed by a deeply Christian vision, and then go out into a secular, materialistic culture, it's easy to see how unfulfilling that is."

A Passion for Food

Like her faith, Ever's passion for food also came from her family. By the time she was born, her father's family had already been in the restaurant business for decades.

"My great-grandfather started the original Colonial Cafeteria in Fort Worth in 1945, and my grandfather inherited it and opened other locations. Patrons would go through the line of homestyle, Southern foods and pick what they liked, beginning with salads and desserts and ending with drinks."

Starting in the '70s, her father managed the family business, where she and her siblings worked from their early teens.

But she also attributes her love of food to her mother, who came from a seafaring family out of Gloucester, Massachusetts, and New Orleans.

"Many of my happiest childhood memories involve my mom or grandmother or aunt at the stove, making 'Chinese rice'—it was leftover rice with egg and bacon mixed into it at breakfast, or shrimp gumbo, or rich chicken curries."

When asked about her favorite foods, fresh fish of the day baked with a buttery crumb topping ranks high.

"When you're up north, you usually make this dish with cod, but you can sub in another white fish or even salmon. You just put the fish in a casserole dish and bake it with butter, herbs, and a topping of crushed crackers."

Besides classic New England fare, she also loves New Orleans-style cuisine, with its Po' Boy sandwiches, oysters, and beignets.

"I still call my mom and ask her how to make family recipes. My siblings do too. At the holidays, you ask Dad for a refresher on cooking meats—turkey or beef tenderloin or ham—and then you get on the phone with Mom to ask details about rice dressing or Brussels sprouts with bacon cream sauce. Faith and food are the major family traditions."

Finding Inspiration (and Love) Abroad

Though Ever comes from a long line of restaurateurs, she never set out to be in the food business. Instead, she started off studying and working in government and international relations, gradually focusing in on Catholic social teaching and how the Church's vision for a culture of life can inform Catholics' engagement with the world.

After graduate school, she spent ten years working for noted Catholic scholar George Weigel at a Washington, DC think tank.

"Part of my job was organizing summer seminars on Catholic social teaching. The seminar leaders had been invited by Pope John Paul II to bring together young people to learn about a culture of life in his home diocese in Krakow. That's where Soren and I met in the summer of 2000."

During the annual program, the American students, who, she notes, all loved their pluralistic country to their core, experienced what it was like to live in a pervasively Christian culture. The students lived in a sprawling Dominican priory dating back to the thirteenth century, in a beautiful town with a gorgeous church on every corner. They worshipped, studied, ate, touristed, sang, danced, and relaxed together with the European students.

"Krakow reminded me of the best parts of my childhood. It was a rich way of life that sprang from gratitude to God. It was full of worship, learning, art, music, good food, and conviviality. It was a lifestyle worthy of human dignity because it was never complete until you shared what you had with people who were different from you, bringing about that sense of mutual respect and community."

Gradually, the Johnsons and Weigel started discussing how they could create such an environment in the United States so that people wouldn't need to travel abroad to experience Christian community and culture. They wanted to respond to John Paul II's call for a new evangelization by helping people experience the Church's vision for the person, family, and community.

In 2006, the Johnsons and Weigel started the John Paul II Fellowship and set about recreating a minor version of the seminar, with Mass, lectures and discussion, dinners and cultural events, all in parishes around Washington. Over several years, they gradually grew a network of John Paul II Fellows. But the temporary nature of the events meant a short-lived experience that took an enormous amount of work to recreate.

Trinity House Café

As the program grew into a separate non-profit, the Johnsons looked for a home base from which to permanently model Christian community and culture and evangelize souls. Ever recalled praying for guidance. Should it be a community center? A business enterprise? And that's when she was inspired to return full circle to the family home-plus-restaurant business of her childhood.

A business would both solve the problem of the temporary nature of the programs they had been doing and would allow access to the public. So they settled on opening a café, a welcoming place where the public can walk into ongoing Christian community and culture. The Johnsons' deepest wish was that they would learn to serve there in a way that would allow their guests to experience God's love.

After raising the capital and doing an area search in Northern Virginia, they found the right setting on Pope Saint John Paul II's canonization day. What they found was a beautiful old home on the corner of Church and Market Streets in old town Leesburg, Virginia. After some legal and financial haggling, the Catholic landlords admitted they liked the idea of supporting such a ministry. It would be a Holy Spirit venture for all involved.

A four-month build-out that included installing a commercial kitchen and replacing all the plumbing ensued, and finally, on October 1, 2014, the feast day of Saint Therese, patroness of missions and one of Ever's longtime intercessors, they opened Trinity House Café.

"This is our response to Pope Saint John Paul the Great's call to bring all the richness of the faith into the public square. We wanted people to see that being a Christian is more than just going to church on Sunday. It's families living out life in the image of the Trinity, an image of communion among persons. They live this 'Trinity House life' with gratitude to God and in accord with human dignity, and they share it with everyone they meet."

Indeed, what guests experience at Trinity House is a beautiful setting with plenty of outdoor seating and dining areas that double as a book and gift shop. Guests relax in comfortable seating to eat, sip coffee, and chat. The walls are lined with art that celebrates both secular and religious themes. Café events include seasonal art exhibits, weekly live music, and occasional book-signings and cultural or children's programs. Every effort they take is to evangelize the culture and bring Christ into the lives of those in their community.

But, of course, one of the main draws of Trinity House is what the espresso bar and small kitchen produce—fancy coffees and teas, breakfast items, sandwiches, soups, salads, and pastries. How about a perfect cappuccino next to a Petersburg salad of roasted beets, goat cheese, and walnuts over mixed lettuces with a tart vinaigrette and toast points? Or the Orleans sandwich of hot sliced chicken, melted cheddar, red onions, spinach, and a divine mustardy sauce on your choice of fresh-baked breads?

Ever says that many guests come from local offices regardless of their faith backgrounds—Jewish, Eastern Orthodox, secular, Protestant of all types, and of course, Catholic.

"Sometimes Christians fear they are not allowed to display their faith in public, but we have found Leesburg to be very welcoming. We love serving the public; it's especially nice to be together with people who aren't just like you. Maybe you get back what you expect from the world."

These days, with her husband finally able to join her in full-time ministry since 2019, the Johnsons are able to do a bit more. Besides managing the café, they are also developing the Trinity House Community of families through "Heaven in Your Home Workshops" and e-letters in which they "inspire families to make home a little taste of heaven for the renewal of faith and culture." After many years of trying to answer the call of Pope Saint John Paul II, Johnson feels she has finally found her way.

Orleans Panini Sandwich

Ever tells us, "This is one of the most popular sandwiches we serve at Trinity House Café. Most of our menu items are named after saints or shrines. And since chicken and mustard are a classic French combo, we named this after the city of Saint Joan of Arc's great victory. This recipe calls for a panini press, which closes over the sandwich to grill both sides at once. However, you can also toast this in a pan on the stove with butter, like making a grilled cheese sandwich. Alternatively, you can make it on toasted bread. It takes about five minutes to prepare and five minutes to cook."

SERVES 1

Ingredients:

- 2 slices sourdough or bread of choice
- Mayonnaise as needed
- Honey mustard
- 2 slices cheddar cheese
- 6 to 8 slices red onion
- 4 ounces sliced cooked chicken breast
- Handful of spinach or other greens
- Butter

Directions:

1. Heat the panini press.
2. Mix desired amounts of mayonnaise and honey mustard in a small bowl and spread on 1 side of each slice of bread.
3. Place 1 slice of cheddar cheese on top of the condiments on each bread slice.
4. Arrange the red onion slices on top of the cheese on one side.
5. Arrange the sliced chicken breast across the top of the onion slices.
6. Arrange the spinach on top of the chicken and close the sandwich.
7. Butter the top slice and place the buttered side down on the panini press. Butter the other side and close the press.
8. Toast until the bread is golden brown, the cheese is melted, and the chicken is heated through.
9. Remove the sandwich from the press, slice it in half, and serve on a plate with a side of salad or chips.

Running
a Polish
Kitchen

Cecilia Glembocki

Easter Eggs at the White House

According to American historians, the beloved Easter egg roll that takes place the Monday after Easter at the White House began in 1878 thanks to then–President Rutherford B. Hayes. Since then, except for several cancellations, the annual event has become a very popular gathering, and at the last public event in 2019, officials estimated that more than thirty thousand parents and children showed up.

Cecilia Glembocki

As one of the volunteers of the event several years ago, Cecilia Glembocki, a member of the Virginia Egg Council, recalls that the children found signed Easter eggs.

"They would run to their mothers to see if they had an egg with the president's signature on the egg. But, lo and behold, they received a congressman's signature or a sports figure's. The moms were not pleased, so since then the only signature on the eggs have been those of the president and the first lady. This tradition has been a favorite for thousands of families."

Growing Up in a Polish Home

Born in Bristol, Connecticut and raised in a Catholic household, Cecilia Glembocki attributes her strong faith to her family. She particularly credits her Polish-born mother, who worked for the Polish consul in New York City. She created a very devout home setting for her family, taking members to Mass, often daily, but always on Sundays and holy days of obligation. She also enrolled her daughter in the St. Stanislaus School in Bristol, Connecticut, where she received a Catholic education.

For Cecilia, however, a major turning point came during her seventh-grade year when one of the school's nuns, Sister Casimir, took her under her wing and guided her through her faith. When she finished eighth grade, she was confirmed, and through this sacrament came to realize the importance of her faith.

"My faith has always been a part of my life. After the eighth grade, I even thought of becoming a nun and visited St. Joseph's Novitiate in Parma, Ohio. But my mother wanted me to finish high school. I loved the formality of religious life and the feeling the Church gave me. The rituals within the Church provide a rhythm to life and a guideline to follow. This is true especially with food."

A passion for food and faith stemmed from her Polish roots.

"In most Polish households, food is strongly connected to faith. This is probably because food and faith are such a strong part of daily life, but also special occasions. I think of Christmas Eve, for example, when we always served certain kinds of food for a big celebration like that. That happened with Easter, too, as we are breaking the Lenten fast. A priest always came to our home and blessed the food at Easter. My mother's goal was always to have a beautiful table and meal for the holidays."

As Cecilia grew older, she began to date, but she remembers finding it hard to be with people who did not understand Catholicism. Until she finally met the right boy.

"My husband, Raymond, had been an altar boy, he was Polish, and he had the same inspirations. He knew all about religion and his family had the same traditions, so we had the same background and values. The transition to married life was so easy because his family shared the same beliefs. It's amazing that these simple traditions, often centered around food, could be something that bound us for life."

The Virginia Egg Council

After marriage, the couple moved from Connecticut to California, then to Florida, and finally to Virginia in 1976 for her husband's new job. While settling down in the area, Cecilia's life was about to enter the world of food in an unexpected way.

It began with her inquiring about a job as a home economist for the Virginia Egg Council,[17] to represent the egg industry and showcase eggs. For her interview, she staged a demonstration for a bridal shower luncheon where she scrambled eggs and served them in a pastry shell with champagne.

The directors of the Egg Council were so impressed that she was hired to represent the egg industry in the greater Washington area and to be a speaker on radio and television shows. She appeared on The 700 Club with Pat Roberts, as well as The Oprah Winfrey show. She even produced her own egg show for a local cable network.

But a much bigger challenge awaited when she was asked to help with that popular White House tradition of the Easter egg roll. Most Americans know that the White House egg roll is an unusual annual event to celebrate a religious holiday, not in church but out in public.

"The first egg roll event I worked on was hosted by Nancy Reagan in 1981. It was such an honor!"

Under the Bush and Clinton administrations, Cecilia proposed to share

---

17 From the Virginia Egg Council website (https://www.virginiaeggcouncil.org/): The Virginia Egg Council is a not-for-profit statewide trade association and has contracted with the Virginia Egg Board to conduct educational and promotional programs, advertise, conduct research, and market eggs in Virginia in cooperation with the Virginia Department of Agriculture and Consumer Services.

springtime traditions of Greeks, Mexicans, Poles, Icelanders, and Ukrainians, plus other nationalities with their egg celebrations. She had participants from those countries come dressed in traditional attire, and the title "Springtime Traditions" welcomed participants who did not celebrate Easter. Representatives from Israel were happy to participate. This way American children could learn of other springtime traditions.

"We started with five countries and moved up to twenty-eight over the years. We shared seder plates, Polish Easter baskets, and toys from other countries."

For thirteen years, she volunteered for many others, showing American children other springtime traditions from many other countries. The rolling of eggs on the White House lawn was an American tradition, but children enjoyed seeing how other families around the world celebrated springtime.

The John Paul II Foundation

Another major focus in Cecilia's Catholic life has been her involvement with the Washington, DC chapter of the John Paul II Foundation.[18] This global organization was established in 1981 by papal decree as a for-profit foundation. Headquartered at the Vatican, the foundation's goals are to preserve and develop the spiritual heritage of Pope Saint John Paul II. It provides a college education, including Catholic teachings, to help young people from former communist countries to return home and lead a Christian life. These students have studied at the Catholic University of Lublin and the John Paul II Pontifical University in Krakow. There are now forty-four chapters of the Friends of John Paul II Foundation in sixteen countries around the world, with fourteen chapters in the United States.

The John Paul II Foundation in Rome welcomes pilgrims from all over the world. The scientific gatherings and meetings devoted to the religious and cultural aspects of the pilgrimage to the Eternal City are held at the Pilgrim's Home. This provides a place where guests experience the religious

---

[18] See https://fjp2.com/foundation-john-paul-ii/.

and cultural aspects of their pilgrimage. Museums located in the John Paul II Foundation Home include about ten thousand gifts that pilgrims presented to John Paul II, all of which have been formally catalogued.

The Washington, DC chapter was founded and accredited within the Washington archdiocese on November 5, 1985. An outstanding member of the Polish American community in Washington at the time, the now-deceased Walther Zachariasiewicz, was the impetus to launch the Friends of John Paul II Foundation in Washington, DC.

John Paul's Polish roots drew Cecilia to the foundation. Her mother used to joke, "He is my cousin!" Though this was not, in fact, true, Cecilia still felt as though the holy pontiff was a part of their family. They loved having a Polish pope to celebrate their traditions and heritage.

As a newcomer, Cecilia told the foundation board that she had some cooking skills that might bring people to the regular meetings.

"I can provide food for your luncheons," she told them. "We can intertwine love and community through the celebration of food."

As a result, she hosted numerous events for the JPII Foundation in Washington. One in particular stands out in her memory, held at the Apostolic Nunciature in Washington. The event, Wadowice-on-the-Potomac, honored Pope Saint John Paul II's fortieth anniversary of his inauguration to the papacy. Wadowice was the Polish birthplace of Karol Jozef Wojtyla, the man who would become pope. At least one hundred people gathered on the ceremonial second floor for a formal meal and speeches by several honorees. Before the meal began, His Excellency Archbishop Christophe Pierre, apostolic nuncio, gave the invocation.

"It was a night I'll never forget. I am so thankful for my time at the foundation."

And clearly the foundation was thankful for her, since she served as its president for four years (while her husband served for another two).

Carrying On Polish Traditions

Looking back over her Catholic life and involvement in the food world, Cecilia realizes that so much of it was shaped by her Polish heritage. To this day, she often cooks traditional Polish dishes and collects Polish cookbooks.

"We now have twelve grandchildren and hope that they carry on the traditions we have tried to pass down to them. My husband and I helped organize the publication of a children's book called *Poland: A Celebration of Traditions and Festivals*. It is a book filled with traditions and customs that still continue in many Polish homes around the world. We run a Polish kitchen and from there, our culture and heritage spreads throughout the rest of the home."

Their book, which has sold copies all over the world, was dedicated to her mother to honor her legacy. "As I look back, I realize what an integral part of family life food and religion are. Having my faith and my family traditions carried me through the death of my parents. Having faith in God when things get hard is the only way to survive."

To this day, Cecilia Glembocki remains the executive director of the Virginia Egg Council and is a member of the Friends of the John Paul II Foundation in Washington, DC. Cecilia and Raymond Glembocki are both recipients of the *Pro Ecclesia et Pontifice* award from Pope Francis for their work on behalf of the John Paul II Foundation. This is the highest award the pope bestows on civilian recipients.

Bigos (Hunter's Stew)

According to Cecilia, "Bigos is almost a Polish national dish, a true staple of any Polish home. We had it in our home, as did Ray's family. There are many versions of this recipe, but this is one of my favorites. It is a very rich and flavorful stew. You can prepare it the day before and reheat it. Some people say it's best after the sixth or seventh day."

SERVES 6 TO 8

Ingredients:

- 3 pounds sauerkraut, rinsed, drained, and chopped
- 15 pitted prunes
- 5 whole allspice berries
- 1 bay leaf
- 1 cup dried mushrooms, soaked in boiling water for 30 minutes
- ½ pound beef stew meat, cubed
- ½ pound pork shoulder, cubed
- ½ pound bacon strips, diced
- 2 tablespoons vegetable oil
- 2 onions, peeled and chopped
- 1 Polish sausage, sliced
- 1 tablespoon caraway seeds
- 1 teaspoon dried marjoram
- Salt and freshly ground black pepper to taste
- ¼ cup red wine
- 3 tablespoons tomato paste
- 20 black peppercorns, optional

Directions:

1. Place the sauerkraut in a large pan or casserole dish and pour 4 cups boiling water over top.
2. Add the prunes, allspice, and bay leaf.
3. Cook over low heat for about 50 minutes.
4. Meanwhile, drain and chop the mushrooms, reserving the liquid.
5. In a separate pot, bring 4 cups of water to a boil.
6. Add the beef, pork, and bacon, and simmer for about 20 minutes until the meat is cooked through, then drain.
7. Meanwhile, heat the vegetable oil in a skillet over medium to high heat.
8. Add the onions and sausage, and sauté while stirring until the onions are soft and the sausage is browned, about 5 minutes.
9. When the sauerkraut is soft, add the drained meat mixture, sausage, onion mixture, and soaked mushrooms; mix well.

10. Cook, uncovered, over low heat, for about 20 minutes.
11. Pour in the red wine and cook for 15 minutes, or until the flavors are well blended.
12. Season with caraway seeds, marjoram, salt, and pepper.
13. Stir in the tomato paste, and black peppercorns, if desired.
14. If the stew is too dry, pour in some of the reserved water from soaking the mushrooms and cook, so the flavors combine for about 5 minutes.

Bigos can be eaten right away, but for a richer flavor, continue to slow cook, covered, over low heat, stirring occasionally. It becomes tastier the longer you cook it. Store leftovers in a covered dish in the refrigerator. Serve with a rich brown Polish Rye bread.

Kremowka Papieska (Polish Cream Cake)

According to anecdotes, this Polish cream cake was a favorite of Pope John Paul II. On a visit in 1999 to Wadowice, his hometown, he told others that this treat had been his favorite since childhood. Once town residents and his followers heard the remark, they renamed the dessert the "Papal Cream Cake," or Kremowka Papieska. Fortunately, it is relatively easy to make, though it must be made a day in advance.[19]

SERVES ABOUT 6

Ingredients

- 1 sheet frozen puff pastry
- 2 cups whole milk
- 1 1-inch vanilla bean or 3 teaspoons vanilla extract
- 6 egg yolks well beaten
- 3/4 cup granulated sugar
- 1/3 cup cornstarch
- Confectioners' sugar for sprinkling

---

[19] Recipe credit: "The Polish Housewife" Lois Britton (polishhousewife.com). Printed with permission.

Directions:

1. Preheat the oven to 425 degrees F.
2. Line the baking sheet with parchment paper.
3. Divide the frozen puff pastry into 2 equal pieces. Poke each at 1-inch intervals with a fork and place on the baking sheet.
4. Top with a layer of parchment paper and an upside-down cooling rack.
5. Bake for 15 minutes, remove the cooling rack and top parchment paper, and bake at least 2 minutes more or until golden brown. Remove from the oven and cool.
6. Pour the milk into a saucepan.
7. Slice the vanilla bean in half lengthwise and scrape out the seeds and add to the milk. Alternatively, add the vanilla extract. Heat the milk until it almost boils.
8. In a bowl, beat the egg yolks and sugar until light and fluffy.
9. Add the cornstarch and mix until well combined.
10. Very slowly, 1 spoonful at a time in the beginning, add the hot milk, stirring constantly.
11. Return the mixture to the saucepan and cook over medium heat, stirring until very thick; some say it should coat the back of a spoon and run your finger through it, it should leave a clear path.
12. Cover with plastic wrap, pushing it down on top of the custard to prevent a skin from forming.
13. Cool to room temperature.
14. Depending on the height of the puff pastry, either use 1 piece as the bottom crust or split 1 and use the bottom half; spread with pastry cream; cover with the top half and press gently. Use a spatula to smooth out the sides, and refrigerate overnight.
15. The next day, cut the pastry into rectangles with a light sawing motion, not with pressure. Before serving, sprinkle with confectioners' sugar.

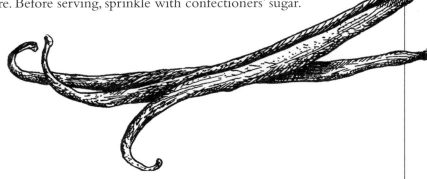

Cooking with a Latino Flare

Rita Steininger

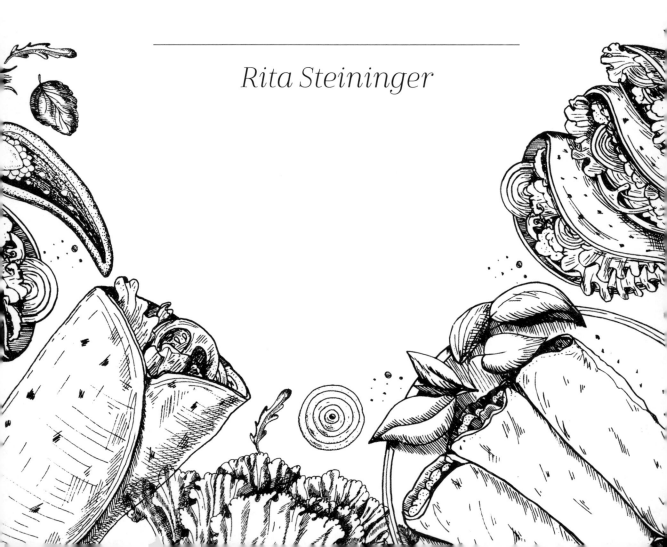

A Home that Proclaims the Faith

Heading up the driveway of Rita Steininger's Northern Virginia home is a little like entering a Catholic retreat center. Wherever visitors look, Catholic images, statues, rosary beads, and paintings all proclaim the homeowners' faith.

Rita Steininger

By the garage door, a carved statue of an angel; at the front door, a three-foot-tall statue of Our Lady, as well as one of Saint Joseph holding the baby Jesus. Upon entering the house, visitors will see three pictures of guardian angels and a large painting of Our Blessed Mother welcoming them to the home. In the living room hangs a large portrait of Our Lady of Guadalupe over the fireplace, and on the mantle stands a carving of Saint Michael the Archangel. In the dining room, visitors encounter a large, silver crucifix from Jerusalem and a silver etching of the Last Supper, also from Jerusalem. And in the kitchen, a three-foot-tall statue of Our Lady holding a beautiful silver rosary, and a large crucifix on the wall decorated with colored stones and put together with two large nails, symbolic of the nails that were used to puncture Christ's body on the cross. And finally, in a secluded area of the garden stands a five-hundred-pound, four-foot-tall statue made of Italian marble and shipped directly from Pisa of Our Lady of Sorrows holding a wreath of flowers and kneeling in prayer.

Some of her most cherished religious artifacts are not displayed but are those she has picked up on her travels, including a collection of rosary beads from abroad. In New Mexico, she bought a beautiful painting on a Mexican tile of the Virgin of Guadalupe. She has also brought back other sacred items from the Holy Land, a spot that remains at the top of her travel list.

One of her most recent trips was to Beirut with her sister in 2019, before the COVID pandemic. She went to visit the church of Saint Charbel to learn of all the miracles people have received and of those who have great devotions to him. Since that visit, she has harbored a strong devotion to Saint Charbel.

Growing in Faith

Although Tom and Rita Steininger are both Catholic, the spirit behind the home's Catholic theme comes from Rita. A native of El Paso, Texas, she attended parochial schools, thanks to her parents desire to pass on the faith to her. She is the eldest of three siblings, with a brother and sister both residing in Denver. Rita has never forgotten her roots in El Paso and still maintains a very close relationship with her family residing there.

Although a practicing Catholic throughout her adult life, Rita became fervent about her faith after a trip in 1993 to Medjugorje, in Bosnia and Herzegovina. Though the apparition has not yet garnered Church approval, Medjugorje has drawn millions of visitors over the decades after Mary apparently appeared to six children in 1981. Her trip there proved to be a defining moment in her faith journey. "The trip was also life changing, and it became a journey back to my Catholic faith from there. After that, I saw life so differently. I felt and feel the presence of God and of the Blessed Mother."

Now Rita has a strong desire to stay close to her faith, adding that she belongs to several rosary groups, including several phone prayer groups (even one in Spanish), and she usually attends daily Mass. Recognizing that many local parishioners were not attending church because of the pandemic of 2020 and all the attendance restrictions, Rita organized a phone group of "Prayer Warriors" and taught them how to call in from their home using conference free call sites.

"The joy of uniting these people of faith through conference calls was a wonderful feeling. I have asked God to please let me be a light to others. I want others to see that light and to be a light for God to help others and to lead them to God. You have to be fed in your faith to grow, and one of the best ways to do that is to surround yourself with people of faith to help you on your journey. It's a journey I've made on my own, and it can be lonely at times, but with the right support, we can persevere."

A Passion for Cooking

While friends, family, neighbors, and fellow parishioners recognize Rita's faith, they also know she is an amazing cook who holds regular dinners, teas, and luncheons, and often hosts dinners for local priests.

"I have always enjoyed having priests over as a way to give something back to them for their service to the Church. And having them in the home encourages me in my faith."

Her passion for cooking began in her childhood while watching her mother, who is of Mexican descent, prepare things in the kitchen.

"My mom was a good cook. I grew up in the kitchen because she was always in the kitchen. I remember coming home and smelling something Mom would be preparing. She was an excellent Mexican cook. There was always the aroma of tortillas, beans, rice, and other typical dishes."

Her mother's influence helped Rita learn more about her Latino culture, both the traditions and the food, as well as the faith.

"I love Latino dishes and culture, but as I grew up and traveled, I got more sophisticated and curious about other cuisines."

One of these other cuisines was Italian, which she became interested in after taking lessons in Firenze, Italy, where she boarded for two weeks with several other men and women and learned cooking from one of the great Italian chefs. Those experiences taught her to enjoy, and even be passionate about, the simplicity of a good meal that uses fresh produce and quality ingredients.

Still more, she learned another valuable lesson. "I learned to enjoy the celebration of life, and that begins in the kitchen. I have a passion for cooking, and I don't know what I would do if I had to stop. I have many cookbooks, and I treasure so much of the history and culture behind them. For me, cooking is an expression of love and care for others."

While it is difficult for her to pick a favorite dish, she admits she must return to her Mexican roots. "If I had to pick one meal that I loved the most, it would be a recipe for shrimp enchiladas (see recipe below). And I think everyone will love making them."

In Love with Our Lady of Guadalupe

Reflecting on her Texan childhood, Rita cannot overlook how important Our Lady of Guadalupe is in El Paso. This probably explains why she has incorporated so many images of Our Lady in her home.

"You see her image everywhere in El Paso, even in grocery stores, churches; she is just everywhere, and you grow up with her. She's our mother. She is part of our culture, and who wouldn't love her once you know about her."

One story in particular exhibits what Rita means about the people of El Paso and their love for Our Lady.

"I remember going to a local butcher's shop to pick up meat for a gathering following my mother's funeral. The butcher was cutting up meat, and I noticed that the back of his shirt had an image of Our Lady. It comforted me during a difficult time. I told him so, and before I knew it, he took it off and gave it to me, only asking in return for prayers for him and his young daughter. That moment stayed with me for a long time. He literally gave me the shirt off his back. I pray for him to this day."

Rita expresses her love for Our Lady by reciting the Rosary daily, and by attending Mass to receive her Son in the Eucharist. And, of course, she adorns her home and garden with statues of her and many other religious items. In all these ways, and by using her passion and talent for cooking, she tries to be a light that leads others to God.

Shrimp Enchiladas con Queso

Rita explains that this recipe can be prepared two hours in advance or even the night before.

"To do so, keep the tortillas and the prepared, cooled enchilada sauce in separate, sealed containers and refrigerate until starting the filling. Remove them from the refrigerator twenty minutes before so they can come to room temperature. Or prepare the enchiladas completely, cover, and refrigerate them until they are ready to bake."

This recipe should serve two enchiladas per person. For lower carbs and even more shrimp flavor, use very thin tortillas and cut them into large rectangles, just shaving off the round edge on opposite sides.

For an extra generous presentation, prepare up to 1 ½ times the enchilada sauce. And for a traditional Mexican feast, serve these with refried beans, guacamole, and a tossed salad.

Note: Rita prefers organic produce and natural ingredients, when possible.

SERVES 6

The Enchilada Sauce:

Ingredients:

- ½ cup unsalted butter
- ½ cup diced red bell pepper
- ½ cup minced onions
- 2 fresh Anaheim chiles, diced, or 1 can Hatch green chiles, chopped, or 2 fresh green chiles, chopped
- 1 medium-sized jalapeño chili pepper, seeded and minced
- 1 garlic clove, peeled and minced
- 1 teaspoon minced fresh oregano or ½ teaspoon dried oregano, crumbled
- ½ teaspoon salt
- Pinch of fresh ground black pepper
- Pinch of cayenne pepper
- 1 ½ cups sour cream or plain yogurt or more as needed
- 2 cups grated Monterey Jack cheese

Directions:

1. Melt ¼ cup butter in a large heavy saucepan over medium heat.
2. Add the red bell pepper, onion, both chiles, garlic, and oregano, and cook until the vegetables are tender, stirring occasionally, for about 5 minutes.
3. Add the salt, the freshly ground black pepper, and the cayenne pepper.
4. Stir in 1 cup sour cream or yogurt and bring to a boil, scraping up any browned bits.
5. Reduce the heat to low and cook for 3 minutes.

6. Slowly mix in 2 cups cheese and stir until melted; you may add more sour cream or yogurt if it is too thick.

7. Remove the sauce from the heat and stir in the remaining ½ cup sour cream or yogurt. Set aside.

The Filling:

Ingredients:

- 1 ½ pounds medium-sized shrimp, peeled, deveined, and cubed into ½-inch pieces
- 12 medium-sized flour tortillas
- 2 cups chopped scallions

- 2 medium-sized tomatoes, peeled, seeded, and chopped or 14 grape or pearl tomatoes
- 2 cups grated Monterey Jack cheese

Directions:

1. Preheat the oven to 350 degrees F.
2. Melt the remaining ¼ cup butter in a large heavy skillet over high heat.
3. Add the shrimp and ½ cup chopped scallions, and cook, stirring frequently, until the shrimp turn just pink, about 2 minutes.
4. Stir in half of the chopped tomatoes and half of the cream sauce.
5. Place each tortilla on a flat surface, and spoon about 1/3 cup shrimp mixture onto each tortilla and trim off the ends.
6. Roll each up tightly, cut in half, and place seam side down in a 9 x 16-inch baking dish.
7. Spoon the remaining sauce over the tortillas, and sprinkle with the remaining chopped tomatoes and chopped scallions.
8. Cover with foil.
9. Bake until heated through, about 20 minutes.
10. Remove from the oven and sprinkle the enchiladas with the remaining 2 cups of cheese and allow to melt under foil more quickly. Serve hot and *buen provecho!*

Cookbook
Authors

"Taboulie"

Julie Ann Sageer

What's in a Name?

Julie Ann Sageer

Imagine that your professional name represents your favorite food. That's the appeal with Julie Ann Sageer, whose childhood nickname became her brand.

"As a little girl, Tabbouleh was the first dish that I helped my mother prepare in the kitchen. I would squeeze the lemons for the fresh juice and pick fresh mint from the garden, and of course I was the taste-tester! One day, my uncle Dominick started calling me Julie Taboulie, partially because I was always helping my mother make it, but I think also because it was a dish that mirrored my personality. Tabbouleh is a fresh, fun, and festive dish that is always on Lebanese tables. So I think in a lot of ways my bright and bubbly personality reminded him of the vibrant dish, plus it rhymes and has a nice ring to it. The name stuck, and my family has been calling me it ever since. So when it was time to create my brand, it was the obvious choice."

Since launching her brand in 2007,[20] this "Queen of Lebanese Cuisine" has been committed to providing a platform for her culture in America and abroad.

"Protecting, preserving, and promoting my beloved Lebanese heritage has been my life's work. I am incredibly humbled and honored to uphold this labor of love."

Acclaimed as the "Catholic Ambassador for Lebanese Cuisine," she credits her deep and devout faith in the Holy Family for this special vocation. From childhood nickname to cooking authority, today she is now known universally as Julie Taboulie, but it would take her belief in her faith to get there.

---

[20] See https://www.julietaboulie.com.

Growing Up in Little Lebanon

As a first-generation Lebanese American, Julie was born in Utica, New York to parents who had emigrated from Northern Lebanon. Utica was heavily populated with other Lebanese, so much so that the town was much like a little Lebanon.

"Our Maronite Catholic church was Saint Louis Gonzaga, where I was baptized. When my family and I lived in Utica, we went to Mass every Sunday, and I remember after Mass joining others to eat *zalabye* (Lebanese fried dough). Its aroma brings back happy childhood memories at church with my family."

Her father, Edward B. Sageer, was a member of the Holy Name Society, a group of devout men who helped build a foundation for the future of Saint Louis Gonzaga Church. Her mother, Hinded, enrolled Julie and her three older siblings in Sunday school where they could learn traditional Lebanese dance. God, the Blessed Mother, and Jesus were always very much present in their home.

"I was always seeing statues, figurines, and iconic artwork of the Holy Family displayed in our home. We were thankful and grateful for God, Mary, and Jesus. My mother often said for us to make the sign of the cross and to let God guide us. 'If it is God's will, it will be.' That's what she told us."

Her mother also regularly told her children to make right choices and to travel down the path God wanted them on.

"'And if not,' she would add, 'God has something better for you.' It was really instilled in me from my mother about offering everything up to God. It gives you great comfort when your own mother says that to you. I am thankful to have a mother in my life with such strong faith."

Julie's mother is a master chef. "The very best Lebanese chef," her daughter claims. "She taught me everything I know. She deserves so much of the credit for my culinary career. I'm so thankful for her."

A Pilgrimage Home

A month-long family trip to Lebanon in 2007 would also play a huge role in shaping her path. Julie admired the devout faith of the Lebanese people, and fondly remembers staying at her grandparent's home.

"My *sitto* (grandmother) was a very holy woman. She had a beautiful statue of the Blessed Mother in her home. Seeing Our Lady displayed in their dining room gave me great comfort. I fell in love with Lebanon on that trip. People don't realize how beautiful a country it is. One of my uncles took me on a day trip to holy sites, and as he drove along the mountain on a long, winding, dirt road, I looked up at the Lebanese mountains, seeing crosses as high as the eye can see. It was awe inspiring to think people climbed to those great heights to honor Our Lord's sacrifice."

She also visited other religious sites, traveling to various shrines, churches, and holy places, such as the pilgrimage site of Saint Harissa, Our Lady of Lebanon, located in Harissa.

"There is a huge white stone spiral staircase that leads up to a fifteen-ton bronze statue of the Blessed Virgin Mary. She is painted white and her arms and hands are stretched outwards towards Beirut. The shrine of Our Lady of Lebanon draws millions of faithful from all over the world."

In addition to touring the holy sites, she and her family also frequented authentic cafés, eateries, pastry shops, and popular bakeries to enjoy traditional Lebanese foods. These epicurean experiences planted a seed in her and foreshadowed her future life.

"When I look back on it all now, it's really interesting because during my stay in Lebanon, I didn't know that I would one day embark on this culinary journey. But I was documenting my travels as if I did."

Julie Taboulie Lebanese Cuisine

After leaving Lebanon and returning to New York, Julie received a God-given epiphany to represent her cuisine, her culture, and her country.

"There is no other way to explain it. It was a gift, and I said yes to receiving it. I knew this was what I was going to do, and ever since experiencing that day of enlightenment, I have been on a mission to do just that. I called my mother and told her, 'Mom, Lebanese cuisine has no representation at this time in America. I know people love Lebanese food and Lebanese people. I am going to represent our culture, Lebanese, and Lebanese chefs and cooks.'"

She decided to move back home with her family in the Finger Lakes region of New York so she could teach people how to make Lebanese food. But first, she herself had to learn how to cook.

"I grew up surrounded by our food, but I really needed to make and master our food myself. And my mother was the source, so I asked her to teach me everything she knew. We went through the repertoire, one recipe at a time. It was more intense because I took learning, teaching, and perfecting the recipes very seriously. Most people think I went to a fancy culinary school, but it was just my amazing mother."

After clocking in countless hours in her mother's culinary school, Julie finally felt ready to start teaching her classes. She officially launched "Julie Taboulie Lebanese Cuisine" in the spring of 2009 with one simple mission statement: to teach people how to make Lebanese cuisine. Just like that the Julie Taboulie brand was born.

She held her first series of hands-on cooking classes and live cooking demonstrations and tasting events at her local library. She was spending a lot of time there developing her brand and series, so when she approached the new director about cooking classes, it was providential that the director was looking for a new program for the community.

The director informed her that there was no kitchen, but instead a large community room. That would be just fine—Julie knew she could convert a room into a fully-functioning kitchen space.

"I set up prep stations and purchased basic cooking supplies and provided tools specifically to prep and prepare my recipes. I started off with a four-week hands-on cooking class series, and to my great surprise, it sold out! We showcased the most well-known Lebanese dishes: hummus, baba ghanouj, falafel, and, of course, tabbouleh. And my mom was right alongside me from day one."

Her students were mostly women (albeit a few gentlemen who came in on occasion) from all backgrounds and nationalities, virtually all with no connection to the Lebanese people.

"My mother and I were offering them a taste of Lebanon right in their own backyard. They were curious about our culture and Catholic faith, and most of all they loved our mother-daughter relationship of cooking and just being together. They really admired our special bond and our back and forth in teaching and storytelling. Our classes would *always* go over time because no one ever wanted to go home."

After just one year teaching there, she launched her popular "Julie Taboulie Lebanese Cuisine" series in New York. As a culinary instructor, she first took her cooking class series to other villages and towns throughout the Finger Lakes region, in Syracuse, and other areas of central New York. Then she broadened her reach statewide with the goal of teaching as many people as possible.

After years of experience, she knew she was ready to launch her cooking classes on television. Fortunately, while in college at Long Island University, at CW Post (today known as LIU Post), she had studied broadcasting communications, where she was taught, trained, and worked as a writer, producer, and host of various campus TV shows. This gave her the necessary skills to launch her own television cooking series.

"I married two of my loves in life: communications and cooking. I couldn't believe it; I was creating, producing, and hosting my very own cooking show. I began by performing live and live-to-tape cooking segments called *Cooking with Julie Taboulie* on local television stations in the area. But then I went statewide to NBC, ABC, and CBS affiliate stations throughout New York."

Today, she has made her mark in the culinary and television world by becoming the first and only Lebanese cooking show in the United States and Canada. Her current cooking show, *Julie Taboulie's Lebanese Kitchen*, airs on PBS and Create TV throughout the United States and Canada.

Julie has also added "award-winning author" to her list of achievements. She wrote her cookbook by the same name, *Julie Taboulie's Lebanese Kitchen: Authentic Recipes for Fresh and Flavorful Mediterranean Home Cooking*, published by St. Martin's Press. Her book won the coveted Gourmand World Cookbook Award for the Best Mediterranean Cookbook in the United States upon its publication in 2017. She is currently working on her next cookbook.

Praised for her "fresh is best" food philosophy, there is one recipe that shall *always* hold a special place in her heart. After all, it's the one dish upon which she's created her entire career.

"My namesake salad, tabbouleh, is truly one-of-a-kind. It's my name and an integral part of my identity. It is such a refreshing, vibrant, and beautiful recipe made with garden-fresh ingredients. It is so colorful, inspiring, and just makes you feel good from the inside-out!"

The secret to making the tastiest bowl of tabbouleh, Julie says, is in the mixing.

"I *always* take my time taste-testing and checking seasonings to achieve the perfect balance of olive oil, fresh lemon juice, and sea salt blended with the fine bulgur wheat, freshly diced ripe tomatoes, spring green onions, and generous amounts of freshly chopped herbs. When you start chopping the freshly picked mint and parsley, the kitchen smells so amazingly vibrant. Mixing by hand is the authentic way to gently toss the ingredients together without weighing them down."

Julie continues, "I *always* serve my tabbouleh in a big, beautiful bowl. That really shows off how fabulous this food really is. And then I love to add fresh sprigs of mint on top and fan out fresh hearts of romaine lettuce leaves spreading them all around the edges of the bowl. You simply scoop up the tabbouleh with the lettuce and eat! That is the Lebanese way."

Every day Julie feels incredibly grateful to God for blessing her with the gifts that he has given her. She knows it was truly God's plan for her to be Julie Taboulie.

"It was not my plan. That came from God, who was preparing me for my destiny."

And she is always grateful to her mother, Hinded, who helped her daughter every step of the way. Still to this day, she is Julie's biggest inspiration and support system. She is also the woman behind the scenes of Julie's cooking shows and cookbook, and travels on the road with her to all of her many appearances throughout the country.

"There is no way that I would be here without her," Julie acclaims. "That much, I am sure of."

Taboulie

The dish Julie wished to share with us is probably no surprise.[21]

"Taboulie is of course one of my absolute favorite things to make and eat—it's a part of my TV name and identity! This refreshing salad of finely chopped vegetables, herbs, and bulgur wheat originated in the area around Mount Lebanon and is an iconic Lebanese dish throughout the world—there's even a national Taboulie day celebrated on the first Saturday of July.

In Lebanese culture, there is no gathering or meal that doesn't feature a big bowl of Taboulie on the table. Although you can eat it with a spoon or fork, I always serve Taboulie the traditional way: with fresh romaine hearts to scoop it up. Chef's tip: the cut matters! Use a sharp serrated knife for best results, and finely chop!"

SERVES 6

Ingredients:

- 3 bunches fresh flat-leaf parsley leaves, finely chopped
- 1/3 cup fresh mint leaves, finely chopped
- 1/2 cup #1 fine bulgur wheat, or 1 cup cooked, chilled quinoa *(for a gluten free version)*
- 4 firm, ripe tomatoes, finely diced
- 6 scallions, ends trimmed, green and white parts thinly sliced
- 3/4 to 1 cup freshly squeezed lemon juice
- 1/2 cup extra-virgin olive oil
- 11/2 teaspoons sea salt
- Hearts of romaine leaves, for serving

Directions:

1. At least 30 minutes before preparing the Taboulie, thoroughly wash the parsley and mint leaves in cold water to remove dirt or debris.

[21] Copyright 2017 by Julie Ann Sageer in *Julie Taboulie's Lebanese Kitchen*, St. Martin's Press/St. Martin's Griffin. All Rights Reserved.

2. Shake out any excess water and drain in a colander, stem sides down.
3. If you have a salad spinner, you can dry the herbs that way or simply lay out on paper towels or a clean kitchen cloth to air dry; just make sure they are very dry before you finely chop them.
4. Place the bulgur wheat into a bowl and cover with 3 cups of cold water. Set aside to soak and soften, about 20 minutes.
5. Combine the tomatoes, scallions, and herbs in that order in a large mixing bowl. By now, the bulgur wheat should have softened. To test, squeeze some of the grains between your fingertips; it should squish and be completely soft. Soak the bulgur longer if needed.
6. Using your hands, squeeze out the soaked bulgur, removing as much excess water as possible.
7. Sprinkle the bulgur on top of the fresh herbs and vegetables in the bowl.
8. Pour in the lemon juice and olive oil, and season with the salt.
9. Toss all the ingredients together (preferably with your hands); it should be juicy but not soggy. Taste and add salt as needed.
10. Serve the salad as soon as possible with fresh, crisp romaine lettuce hearts for scooping.

A
Convert
Cook

Evelyn Birge Vitz

Learning from the Young

"Cooking and baking with children—always such an adventure and a learning experience!" recalls Evelyn Birge Vitz. "Two particular experiences stand out for me."

The first involved baking with her eldest daughter when she was ten years old.

"Rebecca had decided that she wanted to make cream puffs completely on her own, even though I was right there willing to help. The first batch was a flop after she made a crucial error, but she was deter-

Evelyn Birge Vitz

mined to get it right. She immediately tried again, and the next batch was a thrilling success. She showed me, if you care about mastering something, keep trying!"

The second experience came when Vitz was baking many years later with her grandchildren.

"Every Christmastime we have a tradition of baking springerle cookies (more on them to follow) with all the grandchildren I can pull together. My grandson, Simon, has his own personal ritual that day: there is one springerle mold with which he always begins the Christmas baking session: the image of a sleigh ride. I know he looks forward to that ritual all year, and that helps me to appreciate the tradition even more."

Though she has passed on her love of cooking and baking to so many others, these experiences and many others keep her open to learning from the young and the new generations.

A Winding Spiritual Journey

Catholics who love to cook have probably heard of Evelyn Birge Vitz. A convert to Catholicism and a passionate cook and writer, she has shaped her adult life to a substantial degree around her faith, her family, and her interest in food. Indeed, she put all her love for Catholicism and food into her popular cookbook, *A Continual Feast: Celebrating the Joys of Family and Faith throughout the Christian Year.*[22]

"I wanted a book like this, and I couldn't find one. So I wrote one myself. I wanted to explore and to share the wonderful ways that Christians have enjoyed and found meaning in food, over the centuries and around the world."

Now a resident of Northern Virginia, she was born and raised in Indianapolis. Her parents nicknamed her "Timmie" as a baby to avoid confusion with her mother, also named Evelyn. Timmie is still the name she goes by among friends.

Although she is a devout Catholic, she only came to the faith in her late thirties.

"I had quite a religious childhood, a blend of Presbyterian and Episcopalian. I went to church every Sunday and have always had a great love of hymns."

Things changed in her late teens when her father died, and her journey took a darker turn toward atheism. After graduating from high school, she received her BA from Smith College, where she majored in French. She then got a PhD in French from Yale University, becoming a specialist in medieval literature. She accepted a teaching position at New York University (in New York City's Greenwich Village) and became a professor of French. Eventually, she also became an affiliated professor of religious studies, medieval studies, and comparative literature.

---

[22] Evelyn Birge Vitz, *A Continual Feast: Celebrating the Joys of Family and Faith throughout the Christian Year* (San Francisco: Ignatius Press, 1991). Originally published by Harper and Row, 1985.

While at New York University, she met her husband, psychologist Paul C. Vitz. He, too, was an atheist with a weak Protestant background. When they got married, Timmie wore a white lace mini-dress with green shoes and green stockings. Together they wrote their own wedding vows which bore no mention of God. It was far from the traditional wedding ceremony.

But after they had their first child, they decided they did not want to raise their children as atheists. They began to explore their Protestant heritage, and for several years attended an Episcopal church in New York.

But as a medievalist, Timmie had read a great deal about the history of Catholicism and the saints. It became clear to her that she wanted to become a Catholic. Happily, her husband decided the same thing (though for quite different reasons), and they were both received into the Catholic Church at the same time.

As expected, there was an adjustment period. It was a new way of life, neither of them having had any Catholic friends or relatives.

"Fortunately, we had gotten to know some wonderful Catholic priests, and I realized that I loved the Catholic tradition. The more I read, the more I knew I belonged in the Catholic Church. I agreed with the Church's position on all the great issues. It is my natural home. Converting is the best thing I ever did. I am a very happy Catholic."

Deepening Faith through Food Traditions

As for her passion for cooking, that came in her adult years.

"I learned to cook mostly through Julia Child's books while I was in graduate school and early in my marriage."

With the encouragement of an editor at Harper and Row, Timmie began work on a Christian cookbook. Her new faith surrounded and supported this new endeavor.

"I was very interested in the Christian year and the liturgical calendar, and still am. I love to cook, and to try to sanctify family life, to stay focused on faith. All these passions came together in the cookbook."

The purpose of her cookbook is, she said, to help readers appreciate the deep and rich relationship between food and our shared Christian faith. This involves being aware of the richness of the liturgical year—the great seasons of the Christian year and the feasts of saints. Wonderful traditional dishes are associated with each season, each moment. Some traditional dishes are made just once a year for one special feast.

The second aspect she tries to highlight is the dynamic relationship in the Christian tradition between feasting and fasting. There is nothing wrong with enjoying food, and in fact God wants us to, she explains, but we must also know when it is appropriate to fast. While eating is by no means sinful, short-term renunciation of the flesh—in particular, meat—strengthens us against other temptations and allows us to make sacrifices for love of God.

Another aspect she has continually tried to highlight is the importance of family and communal life.

"We want to make our family life, and our meals together, as enjoyable, meaningful, and memorable as we possibly can." Timmie likes to call to mind a quote from the great historian of food Brillat-Savarin: "Tell me what you eat, and I will tell you who you are."

She adds, "Our eating habits should clearly identify us as Christians, indeed as Catholics."

While researching the Church as she considered converting, she learned about the importance of symbolic objects and numbers. For example, many dishes (especially baked goods) are traditionally made in the shape of a cross, or contain a cross within them, for religious holidays. As to numbers, in her cookbook, she provides a recipe for a famous Greek Easter dish made with thirty-three layers of phyllo pastries in honor and memory of the thirty-three years of Christ's life.

Dishes can, of course, draw on many other symbolic and significant numbers, such as three (the Trinity), four (the Gospels), ten (the Commandments), twelve (the apostles), and others. The descent of the Holy Spirit is associated with the numbers seven and twelve, drawn from traditional lists of the gifts and fruits of the Holy Spirit. She provides a cake idea to make with children that encourages them to think about these numbers and what they symbolize. The cake may include a visual depiction of a white dove (the Holy Spirit), yellow rays of light, and red flames, such as those that hovered over the apostles and the Virgin Mary. Food can thus draw on traditional Christian symbols and have valuable catechetical properties—as well as being great fun!

A charming dish that exemplifies the love of symbolism in food is the Christmas stollen. This is a traditional German bread, filled with delicious dried fruits and nuts. The stollen is prepared so that the creases and wrinkles in the bread dough are displayed conspicuously on top of the loaf rather than hidden on the bottom so they won't show. Thus, the top of the cake resembles the swaddling clothes in which the infant Jesus was wrapped.

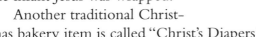

Another traditional Christmas bakery item is called "Christ's Diapers"—these tasty cookies are shaped to look like a baby's diapers. Christmas foods are often, then, intended to remind people of the infant Jesus. Cooking with children at Christmas time is a wonderful way of reminding them of the meaning of the season, and of inviting them to explore, interiorize—and enjoy—Christian symbolism.

"We all want to unite our families—and we can use food to help us draw the family closer together. We want our meals to be happy every day—but it is also true that many of our happiest memories are associated with particular moments of the year."

One of her daughters, while away at college, would make a special trip home each year for Mardi Gras in order to enjoy the traditional and delicious deep-fried apple fritters, made only once on this special occasion.

Writing the cookbook took her several years since a great deal of historical research went into the book. She acquired dozens of cookbooks as she explored the range and richness of the Christian culinary tradition. She is deeply appreciative of the valuable contributions of the Protestant traditions to the Catholic heritage, and they receive acknowledgment in her cookbook.

Now retired from her professorship at New York University, she continues to enjoy cooking and exploring culinary traditions (along with quilting—a new hobby). Among her many favorite dishes is pascha, a primarily Eastern Orthodox Easter dessert made of eggs, butter, cream, farmer's cheese, and plenty of sugar and dried fruits—all the tasty foods that, traditionally, Catholics and Orthodox had given up for Lent but return to on Easter Sunday.

As mentioned, springerle cookies, baked with her grandchildren, are another favorite. These are made using molds that transfer beautifully clear images of all kinds onto the cookies. Some of the images are religious, such as the crèche and scenes from the life of Christ.

"The cookies are beautiful; it's a real art to bake them, and fun."

She also works to keep her life enriched by prayer. She starts each day with a morning offering and the Guardian Angel prayer.

"For many years I have gone to daily Mass. More recently, I have gotten in the habit of reading the Divine Office and Lauds/Morning Prayer, and I read daily from the Gospels. I also pray the Rosary. Starting shortly after my conversion, I had a wonderful spiritual director who encouraged me to do this. It took some getting used to, though, because it was so alien to my Protestant upbringing! I thought my children would hate it and refuse to do it with me—but they really loved it."

"I attempt to make the day and my life as prayerful as I can. I try to keep doing spiritual reading. I am a particular admirer of Ronald Knox and

John Henry Newman. And I stay in touch with fellow Catholics—friendship is very important. We pray for each other. All these things keep us going and enrich us in our faith. To borrow a contemporary (if imperfect) analogy: I try to stay within the powerful divine wi-fi signal."

She also credits grace before meals as a family tradition that enriches the Catholic culture of their home.

"It's a small but important thing we can do to show our gratitude to God for the gift of food."

Timmie and Paul Vitz have been blessed with six children and, at present, twenty-three grandchildren. They are also blessed that one of their sons, Daniel, became a Catholic priest—a very holy one. Fr. Daniel Vitz, IVE, died on Good Friday of 2019 of brain cancer. "It is a great honor—a blessing—to have him as our son."[23]

Timmie feels truly blessed in her faith and to be surrounded by family and friends, in times both difficult and joyous. Family life continues to be a joy for her—as does cooking!

---

[23] A webpage to honor his memory has been set up: http://frdanielvitz.wordpress.com.

Resurrection Rolls

For Easter morning—symbolizing the empty tomb. Christ is risen!

Timmie has decided to share one of her favorite recipes with us.

"This is a wonderful, simple, and meaningful bakery item to prepare with your children for Easter morning breakfast. After being baked, these delicious rolls are empty on the inside (the marshmallows inside disappear in the baking). This symbolizes—and makes visible to children—the empty tomb. Jesus has now risen from the dead! Now, these bakery items are sometimes called 'buns'—but I like thinking of that stone that rolled away from the opening of the tomb, so let's call them 'rolls'!"

Please see below for more beautiful symbolism in these rolls that you can discuss and enjoy with your children.

SERVES 8

Ingredients:

- 1 package refrigerated crescent dinner rolls
- ¼ cup sugar, plus an optional teaspoon or 2
- 1 teaspoon ground cinnamon
- ½ teaspoon grated nutmeg
- 3 tablespoons melted butter
- 8 large marshmallows
- Equipment: a large muffin tin; or a baking dish, lined with parchment paper

Directions:

(and thoughts to accompany them)

1. Preheat the oven to 375 degrees.
2. Unwrap the crescent rolls and separate the sections.
3. Lay each one out on a plate, telling the children that the sheet of dough represents the linen cloth, or shroud, in which Jesus's body was wrapped for burial (see the Gospel of John, chapters 19–20). You can perhaps show your children a photo of the Shroud of Turin, readily available online.
4. Show the children a marshmallow. How white it is! It represents Christ's purity and freedom from sin.

5. Dip a marshmallow in the melted butter, then in the cinnamon and spices mixture—which symbolize the oil and spices that were placed in the burial cloths with Jesus's body.

6. Insert a marshmallow into the center of each roll.

7. Wrap the roll up tightly, pinching it closed. Seal it well (as His tomb was sealed).

8. Continue the process until all the rolls are filled and wrapped.

9. Grease or butter muffin tins. Place the rolls in the tins. If you don't have a large muffin tin, you can use a baking pan lined with parchment paper if possible.

10. Bake at 375 degrees for about 10 minutes, or until nicely browned.

11. Sprinkle with a bit of additional sugar, if you like, or with any remaining sugar and spice mixture—to remind us of the sweetness of our faith.

12. When the rolls are finished and your children take a bite, they will experience that the center of each is empty—as that tomb was empty. Christ is risen!